# ultimate
# CASSEROLE
## book

Publications International, Ltd.

Favorite Brand Name Recipes at www.fbnr.com

Photography on pages 57, 79, 109, 125, 135, 139, 141, 163, 169, 181, 187 and 195 by Stephen Hamilton Photographics, Inc.
**Photographers:** Eric Coughlin, Tate Hunt
**Photographers' Assistant:** Allison Lazard
**Prop Stylist:** Hilary Ashlund
**Food Stylists:** Kim Hartman, Josephine Orba
**Assistant Food Stylist:** Sheila Grannen

**Pictured on the front cover:** Chicken Cassoulet *(page 70).*
**Pictured on front jacket flap:** Sesame-Honey Vegetable Casserole *(page 216).*
**Pictured on the back cover**: Mediterranean-Style Tuna Noodle Casserole *(page 56).*

ISBN-13: 978-4127-2706-8
ISBN-10: 1-4127-2706-5

Library of Congress Control Number: 2007932080

Manufactured in China.

8 7 6 5 4 3 2 1

**Microwave Cooking:** Microwave ovens vary in wattage. Use the cooking times as guidelines and check for doneness before adding more time.

**Preparation/Cooking Times:** Preparation times are based on the approximate amount of time required to assemble the recipe before cooking, baking, chilling or serving. These times include preparation steps such as measuring, chopping and mixing. The fact that some preparations and cooking can be done simultaneously is taken into account. Preparation of optional ingredients and serving suggestions is not included.

# Table of Contents

# Comforting
## Classics

# Chicken Pot Pie

1½ pounds chicken pieces, skin removed
1 cup chicken broth
½ teaspoon salt
¼ teaspoon black pepper
1 to 1½ cups milk
3 tablespoons butter
1 medium onion, chopped
1 cup sliced celery
⅓ cup all-purpose flour
2 cups frozen mixed vegetables (broccoli, carrots and cauliflower),
    thawed
1 tablespoon chopped fresh parsley *or* 1 teaspoon dried parsley flakes
½ teaspoon dried thyme
1 (9-inch) refrigerated pastry crust
1 egg, lightly beaten

1. Combine chicken, chicken broth, salt and pepper in large saucepan over medium-high heat; bring to a boil. Reduce heat; cover and simmer 30 minutes or until juices run clear.

2. Remove chicken and let cool. Pour remaining chicken broth mixture into a measuring cup. Let stand; spoon off fat. Add enough milk to broth mixture to equal 2½ cups. Remove chicken from bones and cut into ½-inch pieces.

3. Melt butter in same saucepan over medium heat. Add onion and celery; cook and stir 3 minutes. Stir in flour until well blended. Gradually stir in broth mixture. Cook, stirring constantly, until sauce thickens and boils. Add chicken, mixed vegetables, parsley and thyme. Pour into 1½-quart deep casserole.

4. Preheat oven to 400°F. Roll out pastry 1 inch larger than diameter of casserole on lightly floured surface. Cut slits in pastry to vent; place on top of casserole. Roll edges and cut away extra pastry; flute edges. Reroll

scraps and cut into decorative designs. Place on top of pastry. Brush pastry with beaten egg. Bake about 30 minutes or until crust is golden brown.

*Makes about 6 cups or 4 servings*

Cook's Nook: 2 cups diced cooked chicken, 1 can (about 14 ounces) chicken broth, $\frac{1}{4}$ teaspoon salt and $\frac{1}{4}$ teaspoon black pepper can be substituted for the first 4 ingredients.

# Tasty Turkey Divan

1 can ($10\frac{3}{4}$ ounces) condensed cream of mushroom soup
$\frac{3}{4}$ cup milk
2 cups cubed cooked turkey
1 package (10 ounces) frozen broccoli florets, thawed
$1\frac{1}{3}$ cups *French's*® French Fried Onions, divided
4 to 5 slices buttered, toasted white bread
1 cup grated Parmesan cheese

1. Preheat oven to 350°F. Combine soup and milk in medium bowl; stir in turkey, broccoli and $\frac{2}{3}$ *cup* French Fried Onions.

2. Place toast slices in bottom of greased 2-quart shallow baking dish, cutting to fit if necessary. Spoon turkey mixture on top.

3. Bake 25 minutes or until mixture is heated through. Sprinkle with cheese and remaining onions; bake 5 minutes or until cheese is melted and onions are golden.

*Makes 6 servings*

Prep Time: 10 minutes
Cook Time: 30 minutes

Comforting Classics

# It's a Keeper Casserole

1 tablespoon vegetable oil
$\frac{1}{2}$ cup chopped onion
$\frac{1}{4}$ cup chopped green bell pepper
1 clove garlic, minced
2 tablespoons all-purpose flour
1 teaspoon sugar
$\frac{1}{2}$ teaspoon salt
$\frac{1}{2}$ teaspoon dried basil
$\frac{1}{2}$ teaspoon black pepper
1 package (about 16 ounces) frozen meatballs, cooked
1 can (about 14 ounces) whole tomatoes, cut up and drained
$1\frac{1}{2}$ cups cooked mixed vegetables
1 teaspoon beef bouillon granules
1 teaspoon Worcestershire sauce
1 package (8 count) refrigerated buttermilk biscuits

1. Preheat oven to 400°F. Heat oil in large saucepan over medium heat. Add onion, bell pepper and garlic; cook and stir until tender.

2. Stir in flour, sugar, salt, basil and black pepper. Slowly stir in meatballs, tomatoes, vegetables, bouillon granules and Worcestershire. Cook and stir until slightly thickened and bubbly; pour into 2-quart casserole.

3. Unroll biscuits; place on top of casserole. Bake, uncovered, 15 minutes or until biscuits are golden. *Makes 4 servings*

# Spinach-Potato Bake

1 pound 90% lean ground beef
1 small onion, chopped
$\frac{1}{2}$ cup sliced fresh mushrooms
2 cloves garlic, minced
1 package (10 ounces) frozen chopped spinach, thawed, well drained
$\frac{1}{2}$ teaspoon ground nutmeg
1 pound russet potatoes, peeled, cooked and mashed
$\frac{1}{4}$ cup sour cream
$\frac{1}{4}$ cup milk
   Salt and black pepper
$\frac{1}{2}$ cup (2 ounces) shredded Cheddar cheese

1. Preheat oven to 400°F. Spray deep 9-inch casserole with nonstick cooking spray.

2. Brown beef in large nonstick skillet over medium-high heat 6 to 8 minutes, stirring to break up meat; drain fat. Add onion, mushrooms and garlic; cook and stir until tender. Stir in spinach and nutmeg; cover and cook until heated through.

3. Combine potatoes, sour cream and milk. Add to beef mixture; season to taste with salt and pepper. Spoon into prepared casserole; sprinkle with cheese.

4. Bake 15 to 20 minutes or until slightly puffed and cheese is melted.

*Makes 6 servings*

# Cajun Chicken and Rice

4 chicken drumsticks, skin removed
4 chicken thighs, skin removed
2 teaspoons Cajun seasoning
$3/4$ teaspoon salt, divided
2 tablespoons vegetable oil
1 can (about 14 ounces) chicken broth
1 cup uncooked rice
$1/2$ teaspoon dried thyme
$1/4$ teaspoon ground turmeric
2 cloves garlic, minced
1 medium green bell pepper, coarsely chopped
1 medium red bell pepper, coarsely chopped
$1/2$ cup finely chopped green onion

1. Preheat oven to 350°F. Lightly coat 13×9-inch baking dish with nonstick cooking spray.

2. Rinse chicken pieces and pat dry. Sprinkle both sides with Cajun seasoning and $1/4$ teaspoon salt. Heat oil in large skillet over medium-high heat. Add chicken; cook 8 to 10 minutes or until browned on all sides. Transfer to plate; set aside.

3. Add broth to skillet. Bring to a boil, scraping bottom and sides of skillet. Stir in remaining ingredients. Transfer to prepared dish. Top with chicken; cover with foil. Bake 1 hour or until chicken is no longer pink in center.

*Makes 6 servings*

Variation: For a one-skillet meal, use an ovenproof skillet. Place browned chicken on rice mixture in skillet, cover, and bake as directed.

# Crab-Artichoke Casserole

8 ounces uncooked small shell pasta
2 tablespoons butter
6 green onions, chopped
2 tablespoons all-purpose flour
1 cup half-and-half
1 teaspoon dry mustard
$\frac{1}{2}$ teaspoon ground red pepper
   Salt and black pepper
$\frac{1}{2}$ cup (2 ounces) shredded Swiss cheese, divided
1 package (about 8 ounces) imitation crabmeat
1 can (about 14 ounces) artichoke hearts, drained and cut into
   bite-size pieces

1. Preheat oven to 350°F. Grease 2-quart casserole. Cook pasta according to package directions; drain and set aside.

2. Melt butter in large saucepan over medium heat. Add green onions; cook and stir about 2 minutes. Add flour; cook and stir 2 minutes more. Gradually add half-and-half, whisking constantly until mixture begins to thicken. Whisk in mustard and red pepper; season with salt and black pepper. Remove from heat; stir in $\frac{1}{4}$ cup cheese until melted.

3. Combine crabmeat, artichokes, pasta and sauce mixture in prepared casserole. Top with remaining $\frac{1}{4}$ cup cheese. Bake about 40 minutes or until bubbly and lightly browned.                     *Makes 6 servings*

Note: This can also be baked in individual ovenproof dishes. Reduce cooking time to about 20 minutes.

# Spicy Turkey Casserole

1 tablespoon olive oil

1 pound turkey breast cutlets, cut into $\frac{1}{2}$-inch pieces

2 spicy chicken or turkey sausages (about 3 ounces each), sliced $\frac{1}{2}$-inch thick

1 cup diced green bell pepper

$\frac{1}{2}$ cup sliced mushrooms

$\frac{1}{2}$ cup diced onion

1 jalapeño pepper,* seeded and minced

$\frac{1}{2}$ cup chicken broth or water

1 can (about 14 ounces) diced tomatoes

1 teaspoon Italian seasoning

$\frac{1}{4}$ teaspoon black pepper

$\frac{1}{2}$ teaspoon paprika

1 cup cooked egg noodles

6 tablespoons grated Parmesan cheese

2 tablespoons coarse breadcrumbs

*Jalapeño peppers can sting and irritate the skin, so wear rubber gloves when handling peppers and do not touch your eyes.

1. Preheat oven to 350°F. Heat oil in large nonstick skillet over medium heat. Add turkey and sausages; cook and stir over medium heat 2 minutes. Add bell pepper, mushrooms, onion and jalapeño; cook and stir 5 minutes. Add chicken broth; cook 1 minute, scraping up any browned bits from bottom of skillet. Add tomatoes, Italian seasoning, black pepper and noodles.

2. Spoon turkey mixture into shallow 10-inch round casserole. Sprinkle with cheese and breadcrumbs. Bake 15 to 20 minutes or until mixture is heated through and breadcrumbs are browned. *Makes 6 servings*

# Apple Curry Chicken

4 boneless skinless chicken breasts
1 cup apple juice, divided
$\frac{1}{4}$ teaspoon salt
   Dash black pepper
$1\frac{1}{2}$ cups plain croutons
1 medium apple, chopped
1 medium onion, chopped
$\frac{1}{4}$ cup raisins
2 teaspoons brown sugar
1 teaspoon curry powder
$\frac{3}{4}$ teaspoon poultry seasoning
$\frac{1}{8}$ teaspoon garlic powder

1. Preheat oven to 350°F. Lightly grease 2-quart baking dish.

2. Arrange chicken breasts in single layer in prepared dish. Combine $\frac{1}{4}$ cup apple juice, salt and pepper in small bowl. Brush juice mixture over chicken.

3. Combine croutons, apple, onion, raisins, brown sugar, curry powder, poultry seasoning and garlic powder in large bowl. Toss with remaining $\frac{3}{4}$ cup apple juice.

4. Spread crouton mixture over chicken. Cover with foil; bake 45 minutes or until chicken is no longer pink in center. *Makes 4 servings*

# Easy Cheesy Ham and Veggie Rice

1 bag (3½ ounces) boil-in-bag brown rice
2 cups broccoli florets
1 cup (3 ounces) matchstick carrots
6 ounces ham, diced
½ cup (2 ounces) Swiss cheese, cut into small pieces
¾ cup (3 ounces) shredded sharp Cheddar cheese
1 tablespoon butter
⅛ teaspoon ground red pepper

1. Cook rice in large saucepan according to package directions. Remove rice packet when cooked; reserve water.

2. Add broccoli and carrots to water in saucepan; bring to boil. Reduce heat; cover and simmer 3 minutes or until broccoli is crisp-tender.

3. Drain vegetables. Stir in rice; heat over medium-low heat. Stir in ham, Swiss, ¼ cup Cheddar, butter and red pepper. Sprinkle evenly with remaining Cheddar; cover and cook 3 minutes or until cheese is melted.

*Makes 4 servings*

To make this dish even simpler, pick up the broccoli florets and matchstick carrots from the salad bar section of your supermarket.

# Split-Biscuit Chicken Pie

$^1/_3$ cup butter
$^1/_3$ cup all-purpose flour
2$^1/_2$ cups milk
1 tablespoon chicken bouillon granules
$^1/_2$ teaspoon dried thyme
$^1/_2$ teaspoon black pepper
4 cups diced cooked chicken
2 jars (4 ounces each) diced pimientos
1 cup frozen green peas, thawed
1 package (6 count) refrigerated biscuits

1. Preheat oven to 350°F. Lightly coat 2-quart casserole or 13×9-inch baking dish with nonstick cooking spray; set aside. Bake biscuits according to package directions.

2. Meanwhile, melt butter in large skillet over medium heat. Add flour; stir until smooth. Add milk, bouillon granules, thyme and pepper; mix until smooth. Cook and stir until thickened, scraping pan with spatula. Remove from heat. Stir in chicken, pimientos and peas. Transfer mixture to prepared dish; bake 30 minutes.

3. Split biscuits in half; arrange cut side down on top of casserole. Bake 3 minutes or until biscuits are heated through. *Makes 4 to 5 servings*

Variations: For a one-dish meal, use an ovenproof skillet. Use whole biscuits instead of halves.

# Shrimp Creole

2 tablespoons olive oil
1½ cups chopped green bell peppers
1 medium onion, chopped
⅔ cup chopped celery
2 cloves garlic, finely chopped
1 cup uncooked rice
1 can (about 14 ounces) diced tomatoes, drained and juice reserved
2 teaspoons hot pepper sauce, or to taste
1 teaspoon dried oregano
¾ teaspoon salt
½ teaspoon dried thyme
  Black pepper
1 pound medium raw shrimp, peeled and deveined
1 tablespoon chopped fresh parsley (optional)

1. Preheat oven to 325°F. Heat olive oil in large skillet over medium-high heat. Add bell peppers, onion, celery and garlic; cook and stir 5 minutes or until vegetables are tender.

2. Reduce heat to medium. Add rice; cook and stir 5 minutes. Add tomatoes, hot pepper sauce, oregano, salt, thyme and black pepper to skillet; stir until well blended. Pour reserved tomato juice into measuring cup. Add enough water to measure 1¾ cups; add to skillet. Cook and stir 2 minutes.

3. Transfer mixture to 2½-quart casserole. Stir in shrimp. Cover; bake 55 minutes or until rice is tender and liquid is absorbed. Garnish with parsley.                                        *Makes 4 to 6 servings*

# Chicken, Asparagus & Mushroom Bake

1 tablespoon butter

1 tablespoon olive oil

2 boneless skinless chicken breasts (about $\frac{1}{2}$ pound), cut into
  bite-size pieces

2 cloves garlic, minced

1 cup sliced mushrooms

2 cups sliced asparagus
  Black pepper

1 package (about 6 ounces) corn bread stuffing mix

$\frac{1}{4}$ cup dry white wine (optional)

1 can (about 14 ounces) chicken broth

1 can ($10\frac{3}{4}$ ounces) condensed cream of asparagus or cream of
  chicken soup, undiluted

1. Preheat oven to 350°F. Heat butter and oil in large skillet until butter is melted. Cook and stir chicken and garlic about 3 minutes over medium-high heat until chicken is no longer pink. Add mushrooms; cook and stir 2 minutes. Add asparagus; cook and stir about 5 minutes or until asparagus is crisp-tender. Season with pepper to taste.

2. Transfer mixture to $2\frac{1}{2}$-quart casserole or 6 small casseroles. Top with stuffing mix.

3. Add wine to skillet, if desired; cook and stir 1 minute over medium-high heat, scraping up any browned bits from bottom of skillet. Add broth and soup; cook and stir until well blended.

4. Pour broth mixture into casserole; mix well. Bake, uncovered, about 35 minutes (30 minutes for small casseroles) or until heated through and lightly browned.                                  *Makes 6 servings*

Tip: This is a good way to stretch a little leftover chicken into an easy and tasty dinner.

# Easy Tuna & Pasta Pot Pie

1 tablespoon butter

1 large onion, chopped

$1\frac{1}{2}$ cups cooked small shell pasta or elbow macaroni

1 can ($10\frac{3}{4}$ ounces) condensed cream of celery or mushroom soup, undiluted

1 cup frozen peas, thawed

1 can (6 ounces) tuna packed in water, drained and flaked

$\frac{1}{2}$ cup sour cream

$\frac{1}{2}$ teaspoon dried dill weed

$\frac{1}{4}$ teaspoon salt

1 package (10 count) buttermilk or country biscuits

1. Preheat oven to 400°F. Melt butter in medium ovenproof skillet over medium heat. Add onion; cook and stir 5 minutes.

2. Stir in pasta, soup, peas, tuna, sour cream, dill and salt; mix well. Cook 3 minutes or until heated through.

3. Unwrap biscuit dough; arrange individual biscuits over tuna mixture. Bake 15 minutes or until biscuits are golden brown and tuna mixture is bubbly.                    *Makes 5 servings*

Prep and Cook Time: **28 minutes**

# Home-Style Shepherd's Pie

Nonstick cooking spray
8 ounces 90% lean ground beef
8 ounces mild Italian sausage, casings removed
1 cup chopped onion
2 cups frozen mixed vegetables, thawed
1 cup water
1 can (6 ounces) tomato paste
$1/4$ cup chopped fresh parsley
1 tablespoon beef bouillon granules
2 teaspoons sugar
$1/4$ teaspoons salt
$1/4$ teaspoon black pepper
$1/8$ teaspoons ground red pepper
1 package (2 pounds) refrigerated mashed potatoes
$1/2$ cup chopped green onions
6 ounces grated sharp Cheddar cheese

1. Preheat oven to 350°F. Lightly coat 13×9-inch baking dish with cooking spray.

2. Coat large skillet with cooking spray; heat over medium-high heat. Brown beef, sausage and onion, stirring frequently to break up meat; drain fat. Add vegetables, water, tomato paste, parsley, bouillon granules, sugar, salt, black pepper and red pepper; stir until well blended.

3. Transfer mixture to prepared dish. Spoon potatoes evenly over top. Sprinkle with green onions and cheese. Coat sheet of foil with cooking spray. Cover dish with foil, sprayed side down, to prevent cheese from sticking. Bake 22 to 25 minutes or until bubbly and cheese is melted.

*Makes 8 servings*

# Indian-Spiced Chicken with Wild Rice

$\frac{1}{2}$ teaspoon salt
$\frac{1}{2}$ teaspoon ground cumin
$\frac{1}{2}$ teaspoon black pepper
$\frac{1}{4}$ teaspoon ground cinnamon
$\frac{1}{4}$ teaspoon ground turmeric
4 boneless skinless chicken breasts (about 1 pound)
2 tablespoons olive oil
2 carrots, sliced
1 red bell pepper, chopped
1 stalk celery, chopped
2 cloves garlic, minced
1 package (6 ounces) long grain and wild rice mix
2 cups chicken broth
1 cup raisins
$\frac{1}{4}$ cup sliced almonds

1. Combine salt, cumin, black pepper, cinnamon and turmeric in small bowl. Rub spice mixture on both sides of chicken. Cover and refrigerate chicken 30 minutes.

2. Preheat oven to 350°F. Spray 13×9-inch baking dish with nonstick cooking spray.

3. Heat oil in large skillet over medium-high heat. Add chicken; cook 2 minutes per side or until browned. Remove chicken; set aside.

4. Add carrots, bell pepper, celery and garlic to skillet; cook and stir 2 minutes. Add rice; cook and stir 5 minutes. Add seasoning packet from rice mix and chicken broth; bring to a boil over high heat. Remove from heat; stir in raisins. Transfer to prepared dish. Place chicken on rice mixture; sprinkle with almonds.

5. Cover with foil; bake 35 minutes or until chicken is no longer pink in center and rice is tender. *Makes 4 servings*

# Pork and Corn Bread Stuffing Casserole

$\frac{1}{2}$ teaspoon paprika
$\frac{1}{4}$ teaspoon salt
$\frac{1}{4}$ teaspoon garlic powder
$\frac{1}{4}$ teaspoon black pepper
  4 bone-in pork chops (about 1$\frac{3}{4}$ pounds)
  2 tablespoons butter
1$\frac{1}{2}$ cups chopped onion (cut in $\frac{1}{2}$-inch dice)
$\frac{3}{4}$ cup thinly sliced celery
$\frac{3}{4}$ cup matchstick or shredded carrots
$\frac{1}{4}$ cup chopped fresh parsley
  1 can (about 14 ounces) chicken broth
  4 cups corn bread stuffing

1. Preheat oven to 350°F. Lightly coat 13×9-inch baking dish with nonstick cooking spray.

2. Combine paprika, salt, garlic powder and pepper in small bowl. Season both sides of pork chops with paprika mixture.

3. Melt butter in large skillet over medium-high heat. Add pork chops. Cook 2 minutes; turn over and cook 1 minute. Remove pork; set aside.

4. Add onion, celery, carrots and parsley to skillet. Cook and stir 4 minutes or until onions are translucent. Add chicken broth; bring to a boil over high heat. Remove from heat; add stuffing and fluff with a fork. Transfer mixture to prepared dish. Top with pork chops. Cover; bake 25 minutes or until pork is no longer pink in center. *Makes 4 servings*

Variation: For a one-skillet meal, use an ovenproof skillet. Place browned pork chops on mixture in skillet; cover and bake as directed.

# Chicken Pot Pie with Onion Biscuits

1 package (1.8 ounces) classic white sauce mix
2³/₄ cups milk, divided
¹/₄ teaspoon dried thyme leaves
1 package (10 ounces) frozen peas and carrots, thawed
1 package (10 ounces) roasted carved chicken breast, cut into bite-size pieces
1 cup all-purpose baking mix
1¹/₃ cups *French's®* French Fried Onions, divided
¹/₂ cup (2 ounces) shredded Cheddar cheese

1. Preheat oven to 400°F. Prepare white sauce mix according to package directions with 2¹/₄ cups milk; stir in thyme. Mix vegetables, chicken and prepared white sauce in shallow 2-quart casserole.

2. Combine baking mix, ²/₃ *cup* French Fried Onions and remaining ¹/₂ cup milk in medium bowl until blended. Drop 6 to 8 spoonfuls of dough over chicken mixture.

3. Bake 25 minutes or until biscuits are golden. Sprinkle biscuits with cheese and remaining ²/₃ *cup* onions. Bake 3 minutes or until cheese is melted and onions are golden.                              *Makes 6 servings*

Tip: You may substitute 2 cups cut-up cooked chicken for the roasted, carved chicken breast.

Variation: For added Cheddar flavor, substitute *French's® Cheddar French Fried Onions* for the original flavor.

Prep Time: 15 minutes
Cook Time: 33 minutes

# Turkey Vegetable Crescent Pie

2 cans (about 14 ounces each) chicken broth
1 medium onion, diced
1¼ pounds turkey tenderloins, cut into ¾-inch pieces
3 cups diced red potatoes
½ teaspoon dried rosemary
¼ teaspoon salt
⅛ teaspoon black pepper
2 bags (10 ounces each) frozen mixed vegetables
⅓ cup milk plus additional if necessary
3 tablespoons cornstarch
1 package (8 count) refrigerated crescent rolls

1. Bring broth to a boil in large saucepan over high heat. Reduce heat; add onion and simmer 3 minutes. Add turkey; return to a boil. Reduce heat; cover and simmer 7 to 9 minutes or until turkey is cooked through. With slotted spoon, transfer turkey to 13×9-inch baking dish.

2. Return broth to a boil. Add potatoes, rosemary, salt and pepper; simmer 2 minutes. Return to a boil; stir in mixed vegetables. Reduce heat; cover and simmer 7 to 8 minutes or until potatoes are tender. With slotted spoon, remove vegetables to colander set over medium bowl; reserve broth. Transfer vegetables to baking dish with turkey.

3. Preheat oven to 375°F. Blend ⅓ cup milk and cornstarch in small bowl until smooth; set aside. Add enough additional milk to reserved broth to equal 3 cups. Heat in same large saucepan over medium-high heat. Whisk in cornstarch mixture, stirring constantly until mixture comes to a boil. Boil 1 minute; remove from heat. Pour over turkey-vegetable mixture.

4. Roll out crescent roll dough and separate at perforations; arrange dough pieces decoratively over top. Bake 13 to 15 minutes or until crust is golden brown. *Makes 8 servings*

# Sausage and Broccoli Noodle Casserole

**1 jar (1 pound) RAGÚ® Cheesy!® Classic Alfredo Sauce**
**1/3 cup milk**
**1 pound sweet Italian sausage, cooked and crumbled**
**1 package (9 ounces) frozen chopped broccoli, thawed**
**8 ounces egg noodles, cooked and drained**
**1 cup shredded Cheddar cheese (about 4 ounces), divided**
**1/4 cup chopped roasted red peppers**

1. Preheat oven to 350°F. In large bowl, combine Alfredo Sauce and milk. Stir in sausage, broccoli, noodles, 3/4 cup cheese and roasted peppers.

2. In 13×9-inch baking dish, evenly spread sausage mixture. Sprinkle with remaining 1/4 cup cheese.

3. Bake 30 minutes or until heated through.          *Makes 6 servings*

Tip: Substitute sausage with equal amounts of vegetables for a hearty vegetarian entrée.

Prep Time: 15 minutes
Cook Time: 30 minutes

This casserole is delicious on its own, but you can make it even better by serving it with a tossed salad and warm, crusty bread.

# Hearty Beef and Potato Casserole

1 package (about 17 ounces) refrigerated fully cooked beef pot roast
    in gravy*
3 cups frozen hash brown potatoes, divided
$\frac{1}{4}$ teaspoon salt
$\frac{1}{4}$ teaspoon black pepper
1 can (about 14 ounces) diced tomatoes
$\frac{1}{2}$ cup canned chipotle chile sauce
1 cup (4 ounces) shredded sharp Cheddar cheese

*Fully cooked beef pot roast can be found in the refrigerated prepared meats
section of the supermarket.

1. Preheat oven to 375°F. Grease 11×7-inch baking dish.

2. Drain and discard gravy from pot roast. Cut beef into $\frac{1}{4}$-inch-thick slices;
set aside. Place 2 cups potatoes in prepared baking dish. Sprinkle with
salt and pepper. Top with beef. Combine tomatoes and chile sauce in small
bowl; spread evenly over beef. Top with remaining potatoes. Sprinkle with
cheese.

3. Cover dish with foil; bake 20 minutes. Remove foil; bake 20 minutes or
until bubbly and heated through. Let stand 5 to 10 minutes before serving.

*Makes 6 servings*

# Salmon Casserole

2 tablespoons butter

2 cups sliced mushrooms

1½ cups chopped carrots

1 cup frozen peas

1 cup chopped celery

½ cup chopped onion

½ cup chopped red bell pepper

1 tablespoon chopped fresh parsley

1 clove garlic, minced

1 teaspoon salt

½ teaspoon black pepper

½ teaspoon dried basil

4 cups cooked rice

1 can (14 ounces) red salmon, drained and flaked

1 can (10¾ ounces) condensed cream of mushroom soup, undiluted

2 cups (8 ounces) shredded Cheddar or American cheese

½ cup sliced black olives

1. Preheat oven to 350°F. Spray 2-quart casserole with nonstick cooking spray.

2. Melt butter in large skillet or Dutch oven over medium heat. Add mushrooms, carrots, peas, celery, onion, bell pepper, parsley, garlic, salt, black pepper and basil; cook and stir 10 minutes or until vegetables are tender. Add rice, salmon, soup and cheese; mix well.

3. Transfer to prepared casserole; sprinkle with olives. Bake 30 minutes or until bubbly and heated through. *Makes 8 servings*

# Louisiana Seafood Bake

1 can (14$^1/_2$ ounces) whole tomatoes, undrained and cut up
1 can (8 ounces) tomato sauce
1 cup water
1 cup sliced celery
$^2/_3$ cup uncooked regular rice
1$^1/_3$ cups *French's*® French Fried Onions, divided
1 teaspoon *Frank's*® *RedHot*® Original Cayenne Pepper Sauce
$^1/_2$ teaspoon garlic powder
$^1/_4$ teaspoon dried oregano, crumbled
$^1/_4$ teaspoon dried thyme, crumbled
$^1/_2$ pound white fish, thawed if frozen and cut into 1-inch chunks
1 can (4 ounces) shrimp, drained
$^1/_3$ cup sliced pitted ripe olives
$^1/_4$ cup (1 ounce) grated Parmesan cheese

Preheat oven to 375°F. In 1$^1/_2$-quart casserole, combine tomatoes, tomato sauce, water, celery, uncooked rice, $^2/_3$ *cup* French Fried Onions and seasonings. Bake, covered, at 375°F for 20 minutes. Stir in fish, shrimp and olives. Bake, covered, 20 minutes or until heated through. Top with cheese and remaining $^2/_3$ *cup* onions; bake, uncovered, 3 minutes or until onions are golden brown.                    *Makes 4 servings*

Microwave Directions: In 2-quart microwave-safe casserole, prepare rice mixture as above. Cook, covered, on HIGH 15 minutes, stirring rice halfway through cooking time. Add fish, shrimp and olives. Cook, covered, 12 to 14 minutes or until rice is cooked. Stir casserole halfway through cooking time. Top with cheese and remaining $^2/_3$ *cup* onions; cook, uncovered, 1 minute. Let stand 5 minutes.

# Beef in Wine Sauce

4 pounds boneless beef chuck roast, cut into $1\frac{1}{2}$- to 2-inch cubes
2 tablespoons garlic powder
2 cans ($10\frac{3}{4}$ ounces each) condensed golden mushroom soup, undiluted
1 can (8 ounces) sliced mushrooms, drained
$\frac{3}{4}$ cup dry sherry
1 envelope (about 1 ounce) dry onion soup mix
1 bag (20 ounces) frozen sliced carrots, thawed

1. Preheat oven to 325°F. Spray heavy 4-quart casserole or Dutch oven with nonstick cooking spray.

2. Sprinkle beef with garlic powder. Place in prepared casserole. Combine canned soup, mushrooms, sherry and dry soup mix in medium bowl. Pour over meat; mix well.

3. Cover; bake 3 hours or until meat is very tender. Add carrots during last 15 minutes of baking. *Makes 6 to 8 servings*

# Fish Broccoli Casserole

1 package (10 ounces) frozen broccoli spears, thawed, drained
1 cup cooked flaked Florida whitefish
1 can ($10\frac{3}{4}$ ounces) condensed cream of mushroom soup, undiluted
$\frac{1}{2}$ cup milk
$\frac{1}{4}$ teaspoon salt
$\frac{1}{8}$ teaspoon freshly ground black pepper
$\frac{1}{2}$ cup crushed potato chips

Preheat oven to 425°F. Grease $1\frac{1}{2}$-quart casserole. Layer broccoli in prepared casserole. Combine fish, soup, milk, salt and pepper in large bowl. Spread fish mixture over broccoli. Sprinkle with potato chips. Bake 12 to 15 minutes or until golden brown. *Makes 4 servings*

Favorite recipe from **Florida Department of Agriculture and Consumer Services, Bureau of Seafood and Aquaculture**

# Mediterranean
## Flavors

# No-Chop Pastitsio

1 pound 90% lean ground beef or ground lamb
1½ cups mild picante sauce
1 can (8 ounces) tomato sauce
1 tablespoon sugar
½ teaspoon ground allspice
½ teaspoon ground cinnamon
¼ teaspoon ground nutmeg, divided
8 ounces uncooked elbow macaroni
3 tablespoons butter
3 tablespoons all-purpose flour
1½ cups milk
½ teaspoon salt
¼ teaspoon black pepper
2 large eggs, beaten
½ cup grated Parmesan cheese

1. Preheat oven to 350°F. Lightly coat 13×9-inch baking dish with nonstick cooking spray.

2. Brown beef in large skillet over medium-high heat, stirring frequently to break up meat; drain fat. Add picante sauce, tomato sauce, sugar, allspice, cinnamon and ⅛ teaspoon nutmeg; bring to a boil. Reduce heat; simmer, uncovered, 10 minutes, stirring frequently.

3. Meanwhile, cook macaroni according to package directions; drain. Place in prepared baking dish.

4. Melt butter in medium saucepan over medium heat. Add flour; mix until smooth. Add milk, salt and pepper; cook and stir 2 minutes or until thickened. Remove from heat. Add about ½ cup white sauce mixture to eggs; stir to blend thoroughly. Add egg mixture to remaining white sauce in saucepan. Stir in Parmesan cheese.

5. Mix about 1/2 cup white sauce into macaroni; toss to coat completely. Spread meat sauce over macaroni. Top with remaining white sauce. Sprinkle evenly with remaining 1/8 teaspoon nutmeg. Bake, uncovered, 30 to 40 minutes or until knife inserted into center comes out clean. Let stand 15 to 20 minutes before serving. *Makes 6 servings*

# Greek Chicken and Spinach Rice Casserole

Nonstick cooking spray
1 cup finely chopped yellow onion
1 package (10 ounces) frozen chopped spinach, thawed and
    squeezed dry
1 cup uncooked quick-cooking brown rice
1 cup water
1/4 teaspoon salt
1/8 teaspoon ground red pepper
3/4 pound chicken tenders
2 teaspoons dried Greek seasoning (oregano, rosemary and sage)
1/2 teaspoon lemon-pepper seasoning
1 tablespoon olive oil
1 medium lemon, quartered

1. Preheat oven to 350°F. Spray large ovenproof skillet with cooking spray; heat over medium heat. Add onion; cook and stir 4 minutes or until translucent. Add spinach, rice, water, salt and red pepper. Stir until well blended.

2. Remove skillet from heat; top with chicken tenders in single layer. Sprinkle with Greek seasoning and lemon-pepper. Cover with foil; bake 25 minutes or until chicken is cooked through.

3. Drizzle oil evenly over casserole. Serve with lemon wedges.
*Makes 4 servings*

Mediterranean Flavors

# Italian Eggplant with Millet and Pepper Stuffing

 1/4 cup uncooked millet
 2 small eggplants (about 3/4 pound total)
 1/4 cup chopped red bell pepper, divided
 1/4 cup chopped green bell pepper, divided
 1 teaspoon olive oil
 1 clove garlic, minced
 1 1/2 cups chicken broth
 1/2 teaspoon ground cumin
 1/2 teaspoon dried oregano
 1/8 teaspoon red pepper flakes

1. Cook and stir millet in large heavy skillet over medium heat 5 minutes or until golden. Transfer to small bowl; set aside.

2. Cut eggplants lengthwise in half. Scoop out flesh, leaving about 1/4-inch-thick shell. Reserve shells; chop eggplant flesh. Combine 1 teaspoon red bell pepper and 1 teaspoon green bell pepper in small bowl; set aside.

3. Heat oil in same skillet over medium heat. Add chopped eggplant, remaining red and green bell pepper and garlic; cook and stir about 8 minutes or until eggplant is tender.

4. Stir in toasted millet, chicken broth, cumin, oregano and red pepper flakes; bring to a boil over high heat. Reduce heat to medium-low; cover and simmer 35 minutes or until all liquid has been absorbed and millet is tender. Remove from heat; let stand, covered, 10 minutes. Preheat oven to 350°F. Pour 1 cup water into 8-inch square baking pan.

5. Fill reserved eggplant shells with eggplant-millet mixture. Carefully place filled shells in prepared pan. Sprinkle shells with reserved chopped bell peppers. Bake 15 minutes or until heated through.      *Makes 4 servings*

# Mediterranean-Style Tuna Noodle Casserole

1 tablespoon Lucini Premium Select extra virgin olive oil

4 cloves garlic, minced

2 large onions, chopped (1$\frac{1}{2}$ cups)

12 ounces mushrooms, chopped (4 cups)

2 large tomatoes, chopped

1 red bell pepper, diced (1 cup)

1 green bell pepper, diced (1 cup)

1 cup chopped fresh cilantro leaves *or* $\frac{1}{4}$ cup dried oregano leaves

2 tablespoons dried marjoram or oregano leaves

1 to 2 teaspoons ground red pepper

1 pound JARLSBERG LITE™ cheese, shredded (4 cups)

1 (16-ounce) can black-eyed peas, rinsed and drained

2 (7-ounce) cans tuna, drained and flaked

6 ounces cooked pasta (tricolor rotelle, bows or macaroni)

Preheat oven to 350°F. Heat oil in large skillet; sauté garlic until golden. Add onions; sauté until transparent, about 2 minutes on medium-high heat.

Add mushrooms, tomatoes and bell peppers; cook and stir 3 to 5 minutes or until mushrooms begin to brown. Add cilantro, marjoram and ground red pepper.

Toss with cheese, peas, tuna and pasta. Pour into greased baking dish. Bake, covered, 45 minutes or until cooked through.

*Makes 6 to 8 servings*

Serving Suggestion: **Serve with crusty bread and homemade coleslaw.**

Mediterranean Flavors

# Spinach Lasagna Alfredo

1 medium onion, diced

1 red or green bell pepper, diced

2 tablespoons olive oil

2 pounds cooked chicken breasts, diced

2 jars (16 ounces each) Alfredo sauce

$\frac{1}{2}$ cup water

1 package (16 ounces) lasagna noodles, uncooked

1 can (27 ounces) or 2 cans (13.5 ounces each) POPEYE® Spinach, well drained

5 cups shredded mozzarella cheese

4 tablespoons Italian seasoning

Preheat oven to 375°F. Sauté onion and pepper in olive oil until tender. Place in large mixing bowl with diced chicken. Add pasta sauce and water to chicken mixture and mix well. Place 1 cup mixture in the bottom of a greased 13×9-inch baking dish. Top with 1 layer of uncooked lasagna noodles. Add $\frac{1}{4}$ of the remaining mixture, layer with $\frac{1}{4}$ of the spinach, 1 cup mozzarella cheese, 1 tablespoon Italian seasoning, and lasagna noodles. Repeat layers 3 times, ending with 1 cup mozzarella. Cover pan tightly with aluminum foil. Bake for 1$\frac{1}{2}$ hours. Remove foil; bake an additional 30 minutes or until cheese browns. Let stand for 15 minutes before serving.          Makes 8 to 10 servings

Tip: For a more traditional lasagna texture, two pounds of browned ground turkey can be substituted for diced chicken.

# Baked Rigatoni

1 pound dry rigatoni
4 ounces mild Italian sausage, casings removed, sliced
1 cup chopped onion
2 cloves garlic, minced
1 can (14.5 ounces) CONTADINA® Recipe Ready Diced Tomatoes,
    undrained
1 can (6 ounces) CONTADINA Tomato Paste
1 cup chicken broth
1 teaspoon salt
1 cup (4 ounces) shredded mozzarella cheese, divided
$\frac{1}{2}$ cup (2 ounces) shredded Parmesan cheese (optional)
2 tablespoons chopped fresh basil *or* 2 teaspoons dried basil

1. Cook pasta according to package directions. Drain and keep warm.

2. Meanwhile, cook sausage in large skillet for 4 to 6 minutes or until no longer pink. Remove sausage from skillet, reserving any drippings in skillet.

3. Add onion and garlic to skillet; sauté for 2 minutes. Stir in undrained tomatoes, tomato paste, broth and salt.

4. Bring to a boil. Reduce heat to low; simmer, uncovered, for 10 minutes, stirring occasionally.

5. Combine pasta, tomato mixture, sausage, $\frac{1}{2}$ cup mozzarella cheese, Parmesan cheese and basil in large bowl; spoon into ungreased 13×9-inch baking dish. Sprinkle with remaining mozzarella cheese.

6. Bake in preheated 375°F oven for 10 to 15 minutes or until cheese is melted.                                      *Makes 8 servings*

Prep Time: 10 minutes
Cook Time: 26 to 33 minutes

# Athens Casserole

2 tablespoons vegetable oil
1½ pounds eggplant, peeled, cut crosswise into ¼-inch slices
1½ pounds ground beef
2 cups chopped onions
1 medium green bell pepper, cut into strips
1 medium yellow bell pepper, cut into strips
1 medium red bell pepper, cut into strips
¼ cup chopped fresh parsley
¼ cup dry red wine
1 teaspoon garlic powder
1 teaspoon ground cinnamon
Salt and black pepper
2 cans (about 28 ounces each) stewed tomatoes, drained
8 ounces feta cheese, crumbled
4 eggs, beaten
½ cup bread crumbs

1. Preheat oven to 350°F.

2. Heat oil in large skillet over medium-high heat. Add eggplant and brown on both sides, 5 to 7 minutes; drain on paper towels.

3. Brown ground beef, onions and bell peppers in same skillet over medium heat. Add parsley, wine, garlic powder and cinnamon; mix well. Season with salt and black pepper.

4. Pour one-third tomatoes into 13×9-inch baking dish. Layer with one-third eggplant, one-third beef mixture and one-third cheese. Repeat layers twice. Pour eggs over top and sprinkle with bread crumbs.

5. Bake 45 minutes or until bubbly and heated through.

*Makes 10 servings*

# Portobello Pesto Pasta Casserole

3 ounces uncooked angel hair pasta, broken into thirds
   Nonstick cooking spray
6 ounces bulk pork sausage
6 ounces sliced portobello mushrooms
1 cup packed stemmed spinach (about 2 ounces)
2 tablespoons prepared pesto
3 tablespoons Italian bread crumbs
1 tablespoon grated Parmesan cheese

1. Preheat broiler. Cook pasta according to package directions.

2. Meanwhile, spray 12-inch nonstick skillet with cooking spray; place over medium heat. Add sausage; cook 4 minutes or until no longer pink, stirring to break up meat. Transfer sausage to plate; set aside.

3. Add mushrooms to skillet; cook and stir over medium heat 4 minutes or until mushrooms are tender.

4. Drain pasta. Toss with spinach and pesto until evenly coated; spread evenly in pie plate. Top with sausage and mushrooms.

5. Combine bread crumbs and cheese in small bowl; sprinkle over casserole. Broil 3 to 4 minutes or until lightly browned. Remove from oven; let stand 5 minutes before serving. *Makes 4 servings*

# Sausage Pizza Pie Casserole

8 ounces mild Italian sausage, casings removed

1 package (13.8 ounces) refrigerated pizza dough

$\frac{1}{2}$ cup tomato sauce

2 tablespoons chopped fresh basil *or* 2 teaspoons dried basil

$\frac{1}{2}$ teaspoon dried oregano

$\frac{1}{4}$ teaspoon red pepper flakes

8 slices smoked provolone cheese

3 ounces whole fresh mushrooms, quartered

$\frac{1}{2}$ cup thinly sliced red onion

$\frac{1}{2}$ cup thinly sliced green bell pepper

$\frac{1}{2}$ cup seeded diced tomato

$\frac{1}{2}$ cup sliced pitted small ripe olives

2 tablespoons grated Parmesan and Romano blend cheese

1. Preheat oven to 350°F. Lightly coat 13×9-inch baking dish with nonstick cooking spray; set aside.

2. Brown sausage in large skillet over medium heat, stirring to break up meat; drain fat.

3. Line prepared dish with pizza dough. Spoon sauce evenly over dough; sprinkle with basil, oregano and pepper flakes. Layer with sausage, provolone cheese, mushrooms, onions, bell pepper, tomato and olives. Roll down sides of crust to form a rim. Bake 30 to 35 minutes or until crust is light golden brown. Sprinkle with cheese blend; let stand 5 minutes before serving. *Makes 4 to 6 servings*

# Midweek Moussaka

1 eggplant (about 1 pound), cut into $^{1}/_{4}$-inch slices
2 tablespoons olive oil
1 pound 90% lean ground beef
1 can (about 14 ounces) stewed tomatoes, drained
$^{1}/_{4}$ cup red wine
2 tablespoons tomato paste
2 teaspoons sugar
$^{3}/_{4}$ teaspoon salt
$^{1}/_{2}$ teaspoon dried oregano
$^{1}/_{4}$ teaspoon ground cinnamon, plus additional for garnish
$^{1}/_{4}$ teaspoon black pepper
$^{1}/_{8}$ teaspoon ground allspice
4 ounces cream cheese
$^{1}/_{4}$ cup milk
$^{1}/_{4}$ cup grated Parmesan cheese

1. Preheat broiler. Spray 8-inch square baking dish with nonstick cooking spray; set aside.

2. Line baking sheet with foil. Arrange eggplant slices on foil, overlapping slightly if necessary. Brush with olive oil; broil 4 minutes on each side. *Reduce oven temperature to 350°F.*

3. Brown beef in large skillet over medium-high heat, stirring to break up meat; drain fat. Add tomatoes, wine, tomato paste, sugar, salt, oregano, cinnamon, pepper and allspice; bring to a boil. Reduce heat; cover and simmer 10 minutes, breaking up large pieces of tomato.

4. Place cream cheese and milk in small microwavable bowl. Cover with plastic wrap; microwave on HIGH 1 minute. Stir until smooth. Arrange half of eggplant slices in prepared dish. Spoon half of meat sauce over eggplant. Sprinkle with half of Parmesan cheese. Repeat layers. Spread cream cheese mixture evenly over top. Bake 20 minutes or until top begins to crack slightly. Let stand 10 minutes before serving.

*Makes 4 servings*

# Chicken Cassoulet

4 slices bacon
$\frac{1}{4}$ cup all-purpose flour
   Salt and black pepper
$1\frac{3}{4}$ pounds bone-in chicken pieces
  2 cooked chicken sausages, cut into $\frac{1}{4}$-inch pieces
  1 medium onion, chopped
$1\frac{1}{2}$ cups diced red and green bell peppers (2 small bell peppers)
  2 cloves garlic, minced
  1 teaspoon dried thyme
   Olive oil
  2 cans (about 15 ounces each) cannellini or Great Northern beans,
    rinsed and drained
$\frac{1}{2}$ cup dry white wine (optional)

1. Preheat oven to 350°F. Cook bacon in large skillet over medium-high heat until crisp; remove to paper towels. Crumble into 1-inch pieces. Drain all but 2 tablespoons fat from skillet.

2. Place flour in shallow bowl; season with salt and black pepper. Dip chicken pieces into flour mixture; shake off excess. Brown chicken in batches in skillet over medium-high heat; remove and set aside. Lightly brown sausages in same skillet; remove and set aside.

3. Add onion, bell peppers, garlic, thyme, salt and black pepper to skillet. Cook and stir over medium heat 5 minutes or until vegetables are tender, adding olive oil as needed to prevent sticking. Transfer onion mixture to 13×9-inch baking dish. Add beans; mix well. Top with chicken, sausages and bacon. Add wine to skillet, if desired; cook and stir over medium heat, scraping up browned bits from bottom of pan. Pour over casserole.

4. Cover with foil; bake 40 minutes. Remove foil; bake 15 minutes more or until chicken is no longer pink in center. *Makes 6 servings*

# Eggplant Crêpes

2 eggplants (about 8 to 9 inches long), cut into 18 ($\frac{1}{4}$-inch-thick) slices
Nonstick olive oil cooking spray
1 package (10 ounces) frozen chopped spinach, thawed and
squeezed dry
1 cup ricotta cheese
$\frac{1}{2}$ cup grated Parmesan cheese
1$\frac{1}{4}$ cups (5 ounces) shredded Gruyère* cheese
Tomato sauce
Fresh oregano leaves for garnish

*Gruyère cheese is a Swiss cheese that has been aged for 10 to 12 months. Any Swiss cheese can be substituted.

1. Preheat oven to 425°F.

2. Arrange eggplant slices on nonstick baking sheets in single layer. Spray both sides of eggplant slices with cooking spray. Bake eggplant 10 minutes; turn and bake 5 to 10 minutes or until tender. Cool. *Reduce oven temperature to 350°F.*

3. Combine spinach, ricotta and Parmesan cheese; mix well. Spray 13×9-inch baking pan with cooking spray. Spread spinach mixture evenly on eggplant slices; roll up slices. Place rolls, seam-side down, in prepared pan.

4. Cover dish with foil; bake 25 minutes. Remove foil; sprinkle rolls with Gruyère cheese. Bake, uncovered, 5 minutes or until cheese is melted. Serve with tomato sauce. *Makes 4 to 6 servings*

# Layered Pasta Casserole

8 ounces uncooked penne pasta

8 ounces mild Italian sausage, casings removed

8 ounces 90% lean ground beef

1 jar (about 26 ounces) pasta sauce

1 package (10 ounces) frozen chopped spinach, thawed and
   squeezed dry

1 cup ricotta cheese

2 cups shredded mozzarella cheese, divided

1/2 cup grated Parmesan cheese

1 egg

2 tablespoons chopped fresh basil *or* 2 teaspoons dried basil

1 teaspoons salt

1. Preheat oven to 350°F. Spray 13×9-inch baking dish with nonstick cooking spray. Cook pasta according to package directions; drain. Transfer to prepared dish.

2. Brown sausage and ground beef in large skillet over medium-high heat, stirring to break up meat; drain fat. Add pasta sauce and mix well. Add half of meat sauce to pasta; toss to coat.

3. Combine spinach, ricotta, 1 cup mozzarella, Parmesan, egg, basil and salt in medium bowl. Spread spinach mixture evenly over pasta mixture. Top with remaining meat sauce; sprinkle with remaining 1 cup mozzarella. Bake, uncovered, 30 minutes. *Makes 6 to 8 servings*

# Pastitsio

8 ounces uncooked ziti or elbow macaroni
1 pound ground lamb or beef
$\frac{1}{2}$ cup chopped onion
1 clove garlic, finely chopped
1 can (about 8 ounces) tomato sauce
$\frac{1}{2}$ teaspoon dried oregano
$\frac{1}{2}$ teaspoon black pepper
$\frac{1}{4}$ teaspoon ground cinnamon
2 tablespoons butter
2 tablespoons all-purpose flour
$1\frac{1}{2}$ cups milk
1 egg, beaten
1 cup grated Parmesan cheese, divided

1. Preheat oven to 350°F. Spray 9-inch baking dish with nonstick cooking spray. Cook pasta according to package directions. Drain and set aside.

2. Cook and stir lamb, onion and garlic in large skillet over medium-high heat until lamb is no longer pink; drain fat. Stir in tomato sauce, oregano, pepper and cinnamon. Reduce heat; simmer 10 minutes.

3. Layer half the pasta in prepared dish. Top with meat mixture, then remaining pasta.

4. Melt butter in medium saucepan. Stir in flour; cook and stir 1 minute. Whisk in milk; cook 6 minutes or until thickened, stirring constantly. Place beaten egg in small bowl; stir some of sauce into egg. Return egg mixture to saucepan; cook and stir 2 minutes. Stir in $\frac{3}{4}$ cup Parmesan cheese.

5. Pour sauce mixture over pasta. Sprinkle with remaining $\frac{1}{4}$ cup Parmesan. Bake 30 to 40 minutes or until golden brown and heated through.

*Makes 6 servings*

# Shrimp and Chicken Paella

$3/4$ cup ready-to-serve rice

2 cans (about 14 ounces each) diced tomatoes

$1/2$ teaspoon ground turmeric *or* 1 teaspoon saffron threads

1 package (12 ounces) frozen shrimp, thawed, peeled and deveined (about 3 cups)

2 chicken tenders (about 4 ounces), cut into bite-size chunks

1 cup frozen peas, thawed

1. Preheat oven to 400°F. Lightly coat 8-inch square glass baking dish with nonstick cooking spray.

2. Spread rice evenly in prepared dish. Pour 1 can tomatoes with juice over rice; sprinkle turmeric over tomatoes. Top with shrimp, chicken and peas. Drain remaining can tomatoes; discard juice. Spread tomatoes evenly over top.

3. Cover with foil; bake 30 minutes. Remove from oven and let stand, covered, 5 minutes.                                    *Makes 6 servings*

Serving Suggestion: Serve with a green salad tossed with mustard vinaigrette and garnished with $1/2$ cup corn.

# Spicy Lasagna Rollers

1½ pounds Italian sausage, casings removed
1 jar (28 ounces) spaghetti sauce, divided
1 can (8 ounces) tomato sauce
½ cup chopped roasted red pepper
¾ teaspoon Italian seasoning
½ teaspoon red pepper flakes
1 container (15 ounces) ricotta cheese
1 package (10 ounces) frozen chopped spinach, thawed and
    squeezed dry
2 cups (8 ounces) shredded Italian cheese blend, divided
1 cup (4 ounces) shredded Cheddar cheese, divided
1 egg, lightly beaten
12 lasagna noodles, cooked and drained

1. Preheat oven to 350°F. Spray 13×9-inch baking pan with nonstick cooking spray; set aside.

2. Brown sausage in large skillet over medium heat, stirring to break up meat; drain fat. Stir in ½ cup spaghetti sauce, tomato sauce, roasted red pepper, Italian seasoning and pepper flakes.

3. Combine ricotta, spinach, 1½ cups cheese blend, ½ cup Cheddar cheese and egg in medium bowl. Spread ¼ cup ricotta mixture over each noodle. Top with ⅓ cup sausage mixture. Tightly roll up each noodle from short end, jelly-roll style. Place rolls, seam sides down, in prepared pan. Pour remaining spaghetti sauce over rolls. Sprinkle with remaining cheese.

4. Cover pan with foil; bake 30 minutes. Remove foil; bake 15 minutes or until bubbly. *Makes 6 servings*

# Easy Moroccan Casserole

2 tablespoons vegetable oil
1 pound pork stew meat, cut into 1-inch cubes
$\frac{1}{2}$ cup chopped onion
3 tablespoons all-purpose flour
1 can (about 14 ounces) diced tomatoes
$\frac{1}{4}$ cup water
1 teaspoon ground ginger
1 teaspoon ground cumin
1 teaspoon ground cinnamon
$\frac{1}{2}$ teaspoon sugar
$\frac{1}{2}$ teaspoon salt
$\frac{1}{2}$ teaspoon black pepper
2 medium unpeeled red potatoes, cut into $\frac{1}{2}$-inch pieces
1 large sweet potato, peeled and cut into $\frac{1}{2}$-inch pieces
1 cup frozen lima beans, thawed and drained
1 cup frozen cut green beans, thawed and drained
$\frac{3}{4}$ cup sliced carrots
Pita bread

1. Preheat oven to 325°F.

2. Heat oil in large skillet over medium-high heat. Add pork and onion; brown pork on all sides. Sprinkle flour over meat mixture. Stir until pan juices are absorbed; cook 2 minutes.

3. Stir in tomatoes, water, ginger, cumin, cinnamon, sugar, salt and pepper. Transfer mixture to 2-quart casserole. Bake 30 minutes.

4. Add red potatoes, sweet potato, lima beans, green beans and carrots; mix well. Cover; bake 1 hour or until potatoes are tender. Serve with pita bread. *Makes 6 servings*

# Lemon Shrimp

1 package (12 ounces) uncooked egg noodles
<br>½ cup (1 stick) butter, softened
<br>2 pounds cooked shrimp
<br>3 tomatoes, chopped
<br>1 cup shredded carrots
<br>1 cup chicken broth
<br>1 can (4 ounces) sliced mushrooms, drained
<br>2 tablespoons fresh lemon juice
<br>2 cloves garlic, chopped
<br>½ teaspoon celery seed
<br>¼ teaspoon black pepper

1. Preheat oven to 350°F.

2. Cook noodles according to package directions; drain. Toss with butter in large bowl until butter is melted and noodles are evenly coated. Stir in shrimp, tomatoes, carrots, broth, mushrooms, lemon juice, garlic, celery seed and pepper. Transfer to 3-quart casserole.

3. Bake 15 to 20 minutes or until heated through.     *Makes 8 servings*

If you don't have any egg noodles on hand, you can use other medium shaped pasta such as rigatoni or farfalle.

# Ratatouille Pot Pie

$^{1}/_{4}$ cup olive oil

1 medium eggplant (about 1 pound), peeled and cut into $^{1}/_{2}$-inch pieces

1 large onion, chopped

1 green or yellow bell pepper, chopped

$1^{1}/_{2}$ teaspoons minced garlic

1 can (about 14 ounces) diced tomatoes with garlic and herbs or Italian stewed tomatoes, undrained

1 teaspoon dried basil

$^{1}/_{2}$ teaspoon red pepper flakes

$^{1}/_{4}$ teaspoon salt

1 tablespoon balsamic vinegar

2 cups (8 ounces) shredded mozzarella cheese, divided

1 package (10 ounces) refrigerated pizza dough

1. Preheat oven to 425°F.

2. Heat oil in large skillet over medium heat. Add eggplant, onion, bell pepper and garlic; cook and stir 10 minutes or until eggplant begins to brown. Stir in tomatoes, basil, red pepper flakes and salt. Cook, uncovered, over medium-low heat 5 minutes.

3. Remove from heat; stir in vinegar. Let stand 10 minutes; stir in 1 cup cheese. Transfer mixture to ungreased 11×7-inch casserole dish. Sprinkle with remaining cheese.

4. Unroll pizza dough; make decorative cut-outs using small cookie cutter, if desired. Arrange dough over top of casserole. Spray dough with nonstick cooking spray. Bake 15 minutes or until crust is golden brown and vegetable mixture is bubbly. Let stand 5 minutes before serving.

*Makes 6 servings*

# Tuna Tomato Casserole

2 cans (6 ounces each) tuna, drained
1 cup mayonnaise
1 small onion, finely chopped
$^1/_4$ teaspoon salt
$^1/_4$ teaspoon black pepper
1 package (12 ounces) uncooked wide egg noodles
8 to 10 plum tomatoes, sliced $^1/_4$ inch thick
1 cup (4 ounces) shredded Cheddar or mozzarella cheese

1. Preheat oven to 375°F.

2. Combine tuna, mayonnaise, onion, salt and pepper in medium bowl; mix well.

3. Cook noodles according to package directions; drain and return to saucepan. Add tuna mixture to noodles; stir until well blended.

4. Layer half of noodle mixture, half of tomatoes and half of cheese in 13×9-inch baking dish. Press down slightly. Repeat layers.

5. Bake 20 minutes or until cheese is melted and casserole is heated through.

*Makes 6 servings*

# Silly Spaghetti Casserole

8 ounces uncooked spaghetti, broken in half
$1/4$ cup finely grated Parmesan cheese
1 egg, lightly beaten
$3/4$ pound ground turkey or ground beef
$1/3$ cup chopped onion
2 cups pasta sauce
$1/2$ (10-ounce) package frozen cut spinach, thawed and squeezed dry
$3/4$ cup (3 ounces) shredded mozzarella cheese
1 red and/or yellow bell pepper, cored and seeded

1. Preheat oven to 350°F. Spray 8-inch square baking dish with nonstick cooking spray.

2. Cook spaghetti according to package directions; drain and return to saucepan. Add Parmesan cheese and egg; toss. Spread in prepared dish.

3. Spray large nonstick skillet with cooking spray. Brown turkey and onion in skillet over medium-high heat, stirring to break up meat; drain fat. Stir in pasta sauce and spinach. Spoon over spaghetti mixture; sprinkle with mozzarella cheese.

4. Use small cookie cutter to cut decorative shapes from bell pepper. Arrange on top of cheese. Cover with foil; bake 40 to 45 minutes or until bubbly. Let stand 10 minutes. *Makes 6 servings*

# Saffron Chicken & Vegetables

2 tablespoons vegetable oil

6 bone-in chicken thighs, skinned

1 bag (16 ounces) frozen mixed vegetables, such as broccoli, red bell peppers, mushrooms and onions, thawed

1 can (about 14 ounces) roasted garlic-flavored chicken broth

1 can ($10^3/_4$ ounces) condensed cream of chicken soup, undiluted

1 can ($10^3/_4$ ounces) condensed cream of mushroom soup, undiluted

1 package (about 8 ounces) uncooked saffron yellow rice mix with seasonings

$^1/_2$ cup water

1 teaspoon paprika (optional)

1. Preheat oven to 350°F. Spray 3-quart casserole with nonstick cooking spray; set aside.

2. Heat oil in large skillet over medium heat. Brown chicken on both sides; drain fat.

3. Meanwhile, combine vegetables, chicken broth, soups, rice mix with seasonings and water in large bowl; mix well. Place mixture in prepared casserole. Top with chicken. Sprinkle with paprika. Cover; bake $1^1/_2$ hours or until chicken is no longer pink in center. *Makes 6 servings*

# Tex-Mex
## *Cooking*

# Creamy Chile and Chicken Casserole

3 tablespoons butter, divided
2 jalapeño peppers,* seeded and finely chopped
2 tablespoons all-purpose flour
$\frac{1}{2}$ cup whipping cream
1 cup chicken broth
1 cup (4 ounces) shredded sharp Cheddar cheese
1 cup (4 ounces) shredded Asiago cheese
1 cup sliced mushrooms
1 yellow squash, chopped
1 red bell pepper, chopped
1 stalk celery, chopped
12 ounces diced cooked chicken breast
$\frac{1}{4}$ cup chopped green onions
$\frac{1}{4}$ teaspoon salt
$\frac{1}{4}$ teaspoon black pepper
$\frac{1}{2}$ cup sliced bacon-Cheddar flavored almonds

*Jalapeño peppers can sting and irritate the skin, so wear rubber gloves when handling peppers and do not touch your eyes.*

1. Preheat oven to 350°F. Melt 2 tablespoons butter in medium saucepan. Add jalapeños; cook and stir over high heat 1 minute. Add flour; stir to make paste. Add cream; stir until thickened. Add broth; stir until smooth. Gradually add cheeses, stirring until melted. Remove from heat; set aside.

2. Melt remaining 1 tablespoon butter in large skillet. Add mushrooms, yellow squash, bell pepper and celery; cook and stir over high heat 3 to 5 minutes or until vegetables are tender. Remove from heat. Stir in chicken, green onions, salt and pepper. Stir in cheese sauce.

3. Spoon mixture into shallow 2-quart casserole. Sprinkle with almonds. Bake 10 minutes or until bubbly and heated through.

*Makes 6 servings*

# Zippy Pork Bake

8 ounces fusilli pasta or other small pasta
1 tablespoon butter
1 teaspoon minced garlic
1 pound ground pork
2 medium zucchini, thinly sliced
1 cup fresh sliced mushrooms
2 tablespoons sliced green onions
1$\frac{1}{2}$ teaspoons chili powder
1 teaspoon salt
4 ounce can chopped green chilies
$\frac{1}{2}$ cup sour cream
1 cup shredded Mozzarella cheese, divided
Browned bread crumbs, optional
Chopped parsley for garnish

Cook pasta according to package directions; drain.

In large skillet over medium-high heat, melt butter; add garlic and sauté until slightly brown. Add pork and cook until no longer pink; about 6 minutes. Add zucchini, mushrooms and onions; cook and stir until tender. Drain.

Stir in chili powder and salt. Add chilies, sour cream, pasta and $\frac{1}{2}$ cup cheese. Pour into 2$\frac{1}{2}$-quart baking dish coated with nonstick spray. Top with remaining cheese and bread crumbs, if desired. Bake, uncovered, in preheated 350°F oven for 20 minutes or until cheese is melted. Garnish with parsley. *Makes six 1$\frac{1}{2}$-cup servings*

Note: This recipe can be made in advance and refrigerated. Bake until heated through.

Favorite recipe from **North Dakota Wheat Commission**

# Fiesta Beef Enchiladas

1 pound 90% lean ground beef
$^1/_2$ cup sliced green onions
2 teaspoons minced garlic
1 cup cooked white or brown rice
$1^1/_2$ cups chopped tomatoes, divided
$^3/_4$ cup frozen corn, thawed
1 cup (4 ounces) shredded Mexican cheese blend or Cheddar cheese, divided
$^1/_2$ cup salsa or picante sauce
12 (6- to 7-inch) corn tortillas
1 can (10 ounces) enchilada sauce
1 cup shredded romaine lettuce

1. Preheat oven to 375°F. Spray 13×9-inch baking dish with nonstick cooking spray; set aside.

2. Brown ground beef in medium nonstick skillet over medium-high heat 6 to 8 minutes, stirring to separate meat; drain fat. Add green onions and garlic; cook and stir 2 minutes.

3. Add rice, 1 cup tomatoes, corn, $^1/_2$ cup cheese and salsa to beef mixture; mix well. Spoon mixture down center of each tortilla. Roll up; place seam side down in prepared dish. Spoon enchilada sauce evenly over enchiladas.

4. Cover with foil; bake 20 minutes or until heated through. Sprinkle with remaining $^1/_2$ cup cheese; bake 5 minutes or until cheese is melted. Top with lettuce and remaining $^1/_2$ cup tomatoes. *Makes 6 servings*

Prep Time: **15 minutes**
Cook Time: **35 minutes**

# Easy Chicken Chalupas

1 fully cooked roasted chicken (about 2 pounds)
8 flour tortillas
2 cups shredded Cheddar cheese
1 cup green chile salsa
1 cup red salsa

1. Preheat oven to 350°F. Spray 13×9-inch baking dish with nonstick cooking spray. Remove skin and bones from chicken; discard. Shred chicken.

2. Place 2 tortillas in bottom of prepared dish, overlapping slightly. Layer tortillas with 1 cup chicken, ½ cup cheese and ¼ cup of each salsa. Repeat layers. Bake casserole 25 minutes or until bubbly and heated through.

*Makes 6 servings*

# Salsa Chicken and Kidney Beans

1 jar (16 ounces) medium salsa, divided
1 can (15 to 16 ounces) red kidney beans, drained and rinsed
4 chicken breast halves (about 1½ pounds)
2 teaspoons chili powder
2 cloves garlic, minced
2 tablespoons sliced or chopped black olives
½ cup crushed tortilla chips
½ cup (2 ounces) shredded Monterey Jack cheese

Pour ¼ cup salsa in shallow 1½-quart baking dish, spreading evenly. Spoon beans over salsa. Sprinkle both sides of chicken with chili powder. Rub garlic into chicken; arrange over beans. Pour remaining salsa over chicken. Cover and bake at 350°F 1 hour or until fork can be inserted into chicken with ease and juices run clear, not pink. To serve, place chicken on serving plate; spoon beans and sauce over top. Sprinkle with olives, tortilla chips and cheese.

*Makes 4 servings*

Favorite recipe from **National Chicken Council**

# Spicy Pork Chop Casserole

Nonstick cooking spray
2 cups frozen corn
2 cups frozen diced hash brown potatoes
1 can (about 14 ounces) diced tomatoes with basil, garlic and oregano,
    drained
2 teaspoons chili powder
1 teaspoon dried oregano
$1/2$ teaspoon ground cumin
$1/8$ teaspoon red pepper flakes
1 teaspoon olive oil
4 boneless pork loin chops (about 3 ounces each), cut $3/4$-inch thick
$1/4$ teaspoon black pepper
$1/4$ cup (1 ounce) shredded Monterey Jack cheese (optional)

1. Preheat oven to 375°F. Spray 8-inch square baking dish with cooking spray.

2. Spray large nonstick skillet with cooking spray. Add corn; cook and stir over medium-high heat about 5 minutes or until corn begins to brown. Add potatoes; cook and stir about 5 minutes or until potatoes begin to brown. Add tomatoes, chili powder, oregano, cumin and red pepper flakes; stir until blended. Transfer to prepared dish.

3. Wipe skillet with paper towel. Add oil; heat over medium-high heat. Add pork chops; brown on one side. Remove pork chops; place browned side up on top of corn mixture. Sprinkle with black pepper. Bake, uncovered, 20 minutes or until pork is barely pink in center. Sprinkle with cheese, if desired. Let stand 2 to 3 minutes before serving.     *Makes 4 servings*

Prep Time: **15 minutes**
Bake Time: **20 minutes**

# Beefy Mexican Lasagna

1½ pounds ground beef (95% lean)
  9 corn tortillas
  2 cans (10 ounces each) mild enchilada sauce
  1 can (15 ounces) black beans, rinsed, drained
1½ cups frozen corn
  1 teaspoon ground cumin
1½ cups shredded Mexican cheese blend
    Crunchy Tortilla Strips (recipe follows, optional)
  ½ cup chopped tomato
  2 tablespoons chopped fresh cilantro

1. Heat oven to 350°F. Brown ground beef in large nonstick skillet over medium heat 8 to 10 minutes or until beef is not pink, breaking up into crumbles. Pour off drippings. Stir in 1 can enchilada sauce, black beans, corn and cumin; bring to a boil. Reduce heat; simmer 5 minutes, stirring occasionally.

2. Spray 11×7 inch baking dish with nonstick cooking spray. Arrange 3 tortillas in dish, cutting 1 as needed to cover bottom. Spread ¼ cup remaining enchilada sauce over tortillas; cover with ⅓ beef mixture, then ⅓ cheese. Repeat layers twice, omitting final cheese layer. Pour remaining enchilada sauce over top.

3. Cover with aluminum foil. Bake in 350°F oven 30 minutes. Remove foil; sprinkle with remaining ½ cup cheese. Bake, uncovered, 5 minutes or until cheese is melted. Top with tortilla strips, if desired, tomato and cilantro.

*Makes 6 to 8 servings.*

Crunchy Tortilla Strips: **Heat oven to 400°F. Cut 1 corn tortilla in half, then crosswise into ¼-inch-wide strips. Place strips in single layer on baking sheet. Spray lightly with nonstick cooking spray. Bake 4 to 8 minutes or until crisp.**

Favorite recipe from **National Cattlemen's Beef Association on behalf of The Beef Checkoff**

# Tuna Quesadilla Stack

4 (10-inch) flour tortillas
$^1/_4$ cup plus 2 tablespoons pinto or black bean dip
1 can (9 ounces) tuna packed in water, drained and flaked
2 cups (8 ounces) shredded Cheddar cheese
1 can (about 14 ounces) diced tomatoes, drained
$^1/_2$ cup thinly sliced green onions
$1^1/_2$ teaspoons butter or margarine, melted

**1.** Preheat oven to 400°F.

**2.** Place 1 tortilla on 12-inch pizza pan. Spread with 2 tablespoons bean dip, leaving $^1/_2$-inch border. Top with one third each of tuna, cheese, tomatoes and green onions. Repeat layers twice, beginning with tortilla and ending with onions.

**3.** Top with remaining tortilla, pressing down gently. Brush with melted butter.

**4.** Bake 15 minutes or until cheese is melted and top is lightly browned. Let stand 2 minutes. Cut into 8 wedges. *Makes 4 servings*

Prep and Cook Time: **25 minutes**

Serve this dish with a salad and chicken tortilla soup for a hearty meal with Mexican flair.

# Cornmeal, Sausage and Chile Casserole

4 ounces uncooked turkey sausage breakfast links, casings removed
1 medium red bell pepper, diced
1/2 cup diced onion
1 teaspoon ground cumin
1/2 to 1 teaspoon chili powder
1 cup chicken broth
1/2 cup uncooked yellow cornmeal
3 egg whites
1 can (about 4 ounces) diced mild green chiles, drained
1/2 cup (2 ounces) shredded Cheddar cheese
3 eggs, beaten
1/2 cup salsa (optional)

1. Heat large nonstick skillet over medium-high heat. Add sausage, bell pepper and onion to skillet; cook about 5 minutes, stirring to break up meat, until sausage is no longer pink and vegetables are crisp-tender. Stir in cumin and chili powder; cook and stir 1 minute.

2. Add broth to skillet; bring to a boil. Gradually add cornmeal; cook 1 minute, stirring constantly to break up lumps. Transfer mixture to large bowl; set aside.

3. Preheat oven to 375°F. Spray 11×7 inch glass baking dish with nonstick cooking spray; set aside.

4. Beat egg whites in small bowl with electric mixer on high speed until stiff peaks form. Stir chiles and cheese into cornmeal mixture. Stir in whole eggs. Gently fold one-quarter of beaten egg white into cornmeal mixture. Fold in remaining egg white. Spoon mixture into prepared dish.

5. Bake 30 minutes or until center is set and edges are lightly browned. Cool slightly. Serve with salsa, if desired. *Makes 6 servings*

# Esperanza's Enchiladas

1 cup vegetable oil

12 (7-inch) corn tortillas, cut into 1-inch pieces

$1\frac{1}{2}$ to 2 pounds ground beef

$\frac{1}{3}$ cup finely chopped yellow onion

1 can ($10\frac{1}{2}$ ounces) enchilada sauce

1 can (8 ounces) tomato sauce

$\frac{1}{4}$ cup water

1 envelope (about 1 ounce) taco or enchilada seasoning mix

2 cups (8 ounces) shredded mild Cheddar cheese

2 cups (8 ounces) shredded Monterey Jack cheese

1 can (6 ounces) black olives, drained and chopped

6 green onions, finely chopped

Sour cream and guacamole (optional)

1. Preheat oven to 350°F.

2. Heat oil in medium skillet over medium-high heat. Add enough tortilla pieces to fill, but not crowd, skillet; fry until crisp. Remove with slotted spoon; drain on paper towels. Repeat with remaining tortilla pieces.

3. Brown ground beef and onion in large skillet over medium-high heat, stirring to separate meat; drain fat. Add enchilada sauce, tomato sauce, water and taco seasoning mix; bring to a boil over high heat. Reduce heat; simmer 20 minutes.

4. Combine beef mixture with two-thirds fried tortilla pieces in large bowl; transfer to 13×9-inch baking dish. Top with remaining one third of tortilla pieces, cheeses, olives and green onions. Bake about 5 to 10 minutes or until cheeses are melted. Serve with sour cream and guacamole.

*Makes 6 to 8 servings*

Hint: Save time by substituting a 1-pound bag of your favorite tortilla chips for the fried tortillas.

# Spicy Beefy Noodles

1½ pounds (90% lean) ground beef
1 small onion, minced
1 clove garlic, minced
1 tablespoon chili powder
1 teaspoon paprika
⅛ teaspoon *each* dried basil, dried dill weed, dried thyme and dried
    marjoram
    Salt and black pepper
1 can (about 14 ounces) diced tomatoes with green chiles
1 cup water
1 can (8 ounces) tomato sauce
3 tablespoons Worcestershire sauce
1 package (about 10 ounces) egg noodles, cooked according to
    package directions
½ cup (2 ounces) *each* shredded Cheddar, mozzarella, pepper jack and
    provolone cheeses

1. Brown ground beef, onion and garlic in large skillet over medium heat
6 to 8 minutes, stirring to break up meat; drain fat. Add chili powder,
paprika, basil, dill, thyme, marjoram, salt and pepper. Cook and stir
2 minutes.

2. Add tomatoes, water, tomato sauce and Worcestershire; mix well.
Simmer, covered, 20 minutes.

3. Combine meat mixture and noodles in 2-quart microwavable casserole.
Combine cheeses in medium bowl and sprinkle evenly over top.

4. Microwave on HIGH 6 minutes or until cheeses are melted.

*Makes 6 servings*

# Mexican Tossed Layer Casserole

1 cup uncooked rice
12 ounces 90% lean ground beef
$3/4$ cup picante sauce
1 teaspoon ground cumin
2 cups shredded Cheddar cheese, divided
$1/2$ cup sour cream
$1/3$ cup finely chopped green onion
2 tablespoons chopped cilantro
$1/2$ teaspoons salt
$1/8$ teaspoon ground red pepper

1. Preheat oven to 350°F. Lightly coat 11×7-inch baking dish with nonstick cooking spray; set aside.

2. Cook rice according to package directions. Meanwhile, brown ground beef in large skillet over medium-high heat, stirring frequently to break up meat; drain fat. Add picante sauce and cumin, stir well. Remove from heat; set aside.

3. Remove cooked rice from heat. Add 1 cup cheese, sour cream, green onion, cilantro, salt and red pepper; toss to blend.

4. Spoon rice mixture into prepared dish. Top with beef mixture. Cover with foil; bake 20 minutes or until heated through. Sprinkle with remaining cheese. Bake, uncovered, 3 minutes or until cheese is melted.

*Makes 4 servings*

# Chili Beef and Corn Casserole

   Nonstick cooking spray
$3/4$ pound 90% lean ground beef
$1/4$ cup salsa
   2 teaspoons chili powder
$1\frac{1}{2}$ teaspoons ground cumin
   2 cups frozen corn kernels, thawed
   2 ounces chopped collard greens, about $1/2$-inch pieces (1 cup packed)
$1/2$ cup sour cream
$1/4$ cup (1 ounce) shredded sharp Cheddar cheese

1. Preheat oven 350°F.

2. Coat 12-inch nonstick skillet with cooking spray. Brown ground beef over medium-high heat 6 to 8 minutes, stirring to break up meat; drain fat. Add salsa, chili powder and cumin; cook and stir 1 minute. Remove from heat.

3. Coat 8-inch square baking pan with cooking spray. Combine corn and collard greens in pan; toss to blend. Spoon beef mixture evenly over vegetables. Cover with foil; bake 25 minutes or until greens are tender.

4. Top each serving with 2 tablespoons sour cream and 1 tablespoon shredded cheese.                    *Makes 4 servings*

# Cerveza Chicken Enchilada Casserole

2 cups water

1 stalk celery, chopped

1 small carrot, chopped

1 bottle (12 ounces) Mexican beer, divided

Juice of 1 lime

1 teaspoon salt

1½ pounds boneless skinless chicken breasts

1 can (19 ounces) enchilada sauce

7 ounces white corn tortilla chips

½ medium onion, chopped

3 cups shredded Cheddar cheese

Sour cream, sliced olives and cilantro (optional)

**Slow Cooker Directions**

1. Bring water, celery, carrot, 1 cup beer, lime juice and salt to a boil in large saucepan over high heat. Add chicken breasts; reduce heat and simmer. Cook until chicken about 12 to 14 minutes or until no longer pink in center. Remove; cool and shred chicken.

2. Spoon ½ cup enchilada sauce in 5-quart slow cooker. Sprinkle tortilla chips evenly over sauce. Cover with one-third shredded chicken. Sprinkle one-third chopped onion over chicken. Sprinkle with 1 cup cheese. Pour ½ cup enchilada sauce over cheese. Repeat layers, pouring remaining beer over casserole before adding last layer of cheese.

3. Cover; cook on LOW 3½ to 4 hours. Garnish with sour cream, sliced olives and cilantro, if desired. *Makes 4 to 6 servings*

# Tortilla Beef Casserole

1 package (about 17 ounces) refrigerated fully cooked beef pot roast in gravy*

6 (6-inch) corn tortillas, cut into 1-inch pieces

1 jar (16 ounces) salsa

1½ cups canned or frozen corn

1 cup black or pinto beans, rinsed and drained

1 cup (4 ounces) shredded Mexican cheese blend

*Fully cooked beef pot roast can be found in the refrigerated prepared meats section of the supermarket.*

1. Preheat oven to 350°F. Lightly spray 2-quart casserole with nonstick cooking spray.

2. Drain and discard gravy from pot roast; cut or shred beef into bite-size pieces.

3. Combine beef, tortillas, salsa, corn and beans in large bowl; mix well. Transfer to prepared casserole. Bake 20 minutes or until heated through. Sprinkle with cheese; bake 5 minutes or until cheese is melted.

*Makes 4 servings*

 Tip

Mexican cheese blend is a combination of pepper jack cheese, Cheddar cheese with bits of jalapeño pepper or ground spices such as chili powder.

# Cheesy Chicken Enchiladas

$^{1}/_{4}$ cup ($^{1}/_{2}$ stick) butter
1 cup chopped onion
2 cloves garlic, minced
$^{1}/_{4}$ cup all-purpose flour
1 cup chicken broth
4 ounces cream cheese, softened
2 cups (8 ounces) shredded Mexican cheese blend, divided
1 cup shredded cooked chicken
1 can (7 ounces) diced mild green chiles, drained
$^{1}/_{2}$ cup diced pimientos
6 (8-inch) flour tortillas, warmed
$^{1}/_{4}$ cup chopped fresh cilantro
$^{3}/_{4}$ cup salsa

1. Preheat oven to 350°F. Spray 13×9-inch baking dish with nonstick cooking spray.

2. Melt butter in medium saucepan over medium heat. Add onion and garlic; cook and stir until onion is tender. Add flour; cook and stir 1 minute. Gradually add chicken broth; cook and stir 2 to 3 minutes or until slightly thickened. Add cream cheese; stir until melted. Stir in $^{1}/_{2}$ cup shredded cheese, chicken, chiles and pimientos.

3. Spoon about $^{1}/_{3}$ cup mixture down center of each tortilla. Roll up and place seam side down in prepared baking dish. Pour remaining mixture over enchiladas; sprinkle with remaining $1^{1}/_{2}$ cups shredded cheese.

4. Bake 20 minutes or until bubbly and lightly browned. Sprinkle with cilantro. Serve with salsa. *Makes 6 servings*

# Tamale Pie

1 tablespoon vegetable oil
$1/2$ cup chopped onion
$1/3$ cup chopped red bell pepper
1 clove garlic, minced
$3/4$ pound ground turkey
$3/4$ teaspoon chili powder
$1/2$ teaspoon dried oregano
1 can (about 14 ounces) Mexican-style stewed tomatoes, undrained
1 can (about 15 ounces) chili beans in mild chili sauce, undrained
1 cup corn
$1/4$ teaspoon black pepper
1 package ($8^1/2$ ounces) corn muffin mix plus ingredients to
    prepare mix
2 cups taco-flavored shredded cheese, divided

1. Heat oil in large skillet over medium heat. Add onion and bell pepper; cook until crisp-tender. Stir in garlic. Add turkey; cook until turkey is no longer pink, stirring occasionally. Stir in chili powder and oregano. Add tomatoes; cook and stir 2 minutes, breaking up tomatoes with spoon. Stir in beans, corn and black pepper; simmer 10 minutes or until liquid is reduced by about half.

2. Preheat oven to 375°F. Lightly grease $1^1/2$- to 2-quart casserole. Prepare corn muffin mix according to package directions; stir in $1/2$ cup cheese.

3. Spread half of turkey mixture in prepared casserole; sprinkle with $3/4$ cup cheese. Top with remaining turkey mixture and $3/4$ cup cheese. Top with corn muffin batter. Bake 20 to 22 minutes or until light golden brown.

*Makes 3 to 4 servings*

# Southwestern Enchiladas

1 can (10 ounces) enchilada sauce, divided
2 packages (about 6 ounces each) refrigerated fully cooked steak
    strips*
4 (8-inch) flour tortillas
1/2 cup condensed nacho cheese soup, undiluted
1 1/2 cups (6 ounces) shredded Mexican cheese blend

*Fully cooked steak strips can be found in the refrigerated prepared meats section of the supermarket.*

**1.** Preheat oven to 350°F. Spread half of enchilada sauce in 9-inch baking dish; set aside.

**2.** Place about 3 ounces steak down center of each tortilla. Top with 2 tablespoons cheese soup. Roll up tortillas; place seam side down in dish. Pour remaining enchilada sauce evenly over tortillas. Sprinkle with cheese. Bake 20 to 25 minutes or until heated through. *Makes 4 servings*

Instead of using condensed nacho cheese soup in this recipe, try substituting 1/2 cup chile-flavored pasteurized processed cheese spread for a change of pace.

Tex-Mex Cooking

# Chili Cheese Puff

3/4 cup all-purpose flour
1 1/2 teaspoons baking powder
9 eggs
4 cups (16 ounces) shredded Monterey Jack cheese
2 cups (16 ounces) cottage cheese
2 cans (4 ounces each) diced green chiles, drained
1 1/2 teaspoons sugar
1/4 teaspoon salt
Dash hot pepper sauce
1 cup salsa

**1.** Preheat oven to 350°F. Spray 13×9-inch baking dish with nonstick cooking spray.

**2.** Combine flour and baking powder in small bowl. Whisk eggs in large bowl; stir in Monterey Jack, cottage cheese, chiles, sugar, salt and hot pepper sauce. Add flour mixture; stir just until blended. Pour into prepared dish.

**3.** Bake, uncovered, 45 minutes or until set. Let stand 5 minutes before serving. Serve with salsa. *Makes 8 servings*

# Mexican Lasagna

1 jar (1 pound 10 ounces) RAGÚ® Old World Style® Pasta Sauce
1 pound ground beef
1 can (15¼ ounces) whole kernel corn, drained
4½ teaspoons chili powder
6 (8½-inch) flour tortillas
2 cups shredded Cheddar cheese (about 8 ounces)

**1.** Preheat oven to 350°F. Set aside 1 cup Ragú Pasta Sauce. In 10-inch skillet, brown ground beef over medium-high heat; drain. Stir in remaining Ragú Pasta Sauce, corn and chili powder.

**2.** In 13×9-inch baking dish, spread 1 cup sauce mixture. Arrange two tortillas over sauce, overlapping edges slightly. Layer half the sauce mixture and ⅓ of the cheese over tortillas; repeat layers, ending with tortillas. Spread tortillas with reserved sauce.

**3.** Bake 30 minutes, then top with remaining cheese and bake an additional 10 minutes or until sauce is bubbling and cheese is melted.

*Makes 8 servings*

Tip: Substitute refried beans for ground beef for a meatless main dish.

Prep Time: **10 minutes**
Cook Time: **40 minutes**

# Spicy Chicken Tortilla Casserole

1 tablespoon vegetable oil
1 cup chopped green bell pepper
1 small onion, chopped
2 cloves garlic, finely chopped
1 pound (about 4) boneless, skinless chicken breast halves, cut into
bite-size pieces
1 jar (16 ounces) ORTEGA® Salsa, any variety
1 can (2.25 ounces) sliced ripe olives
6 corn tortillas, cut into halves
2 cups (8 ounces) shredded Monterey Jack or cheddar cheese
Sour cream (optional)

**PREHEAT** oven to 350°F.

**HEAT** oil in large skillet over medium-high heat. Add bell pepper, onion and garlic; cook for 2 to 3 minutes or until vegetables are tender.

**ADD** chicken; cook, stirring frequently, for 3 to 5 minutes or until chicken is no longer pink in center. Stir in salsa and olives; remove from heat.

**PLACE** 6 tortilla halves onto bottom of ungreased 8-inch square baking pan. Top with half of chicken mixture and 1 cup cheese; repeat.

**BAKE** for 15 to 20 minutes or until bubbly. Serve with sour cream.

*Makes 8 servings*

# Brunch-Time
## *Favorites*

# Crustless Salmon & Broccoli Quiche

3 eggs *or* ¾ cup cholesterol-free egg substitute

¼ cup chopped green onions

¼ cup plain yogurt

2 teaspoons flour

1 teaspoon dried basil

⅛ teaspoon salt

⅛ teaspoon black pepper

¾ cup broccoli florets

⅓ cup (3 ounces) drained and flaked water-packed boneless skinless canned salmon

2 tablespoons grated Parmesan cheese

1 plum tomato, thinly sliced

¼ cup fresh bread crumbs

1. Preheat oven to 375°F. Spray 9-inch pie plate or 2-quart casserole with nonstick cooking spray.

2. Combine eggs, green onions, yogurt, flour, basil, salt and pepper in medium bowl until well blended. Stir in broccoli, salmon and cheese. Spread evenly in prepared casserole. Top with tomato slices; sprinkle with bread crumbs.

3. Bake, uncovered, 20 to 25 minutes or until knife inserted into center comes out clean. Let stand 5 minutes.               *Makes 2 servings*

# Easy Crab-Asparagus Pie

4 ounces crabmeat, shell and cartilage removed, flaked

1$\frac{1}{2}$ cups sliced cooked asparagus

$\frac{1}{2}$ cup chopped onion, cooked

1 cup (4 ounces) shredded Monterey Jack cheese

$\frac{1}{4}$ cup (1 ounce) grated Parmesan cheese

Black pepper

$\frac{3}{4}$ cup all-purpose flour

$\frac{3}{4}$ teaspoon baking powder

$\frac{1}{2}$ teaspoon salt

2 tablespoons butter or margarine, chilled

1$\frac{1}{2}$ cups milk

4 eggs, lightly beaten

1. Preheat oven to 350°F. Lightly grease pie plate or 10-inch quiche dish.

2. Layer crabmeat, asparagus and onion in prepared dish; top with cheeses. Season with pepper.

3. Combine flour, baking powder and salt in large bowl. Cut in butter with pastry blender or 2 knives until mixture forms coarse crumbs. Stir in milk and eggs; pour into pie plate.

4. Bake 30 minutes or until filling is puffed and knife inserted into center comes out clean.                     *Makes 6 servings*

# Chipotle Turkey Strata

6 to 8 ($\frac{1}{2}$-inch-thick) Italian bread slices

2 tablespoons chipotle sauce*

2 cups chopped cooked dark turkey meat

$1\frac{1}{2}$ cups (12 ounces) shredded Cheddar cheese, divided

$2\frac{1}{2}$ cups milk

5 eggs

$\frac{1}{2}$ teaspoon salt

$\frac{1}{4}$ teaspoon pepper

*If you can't find chipotle sauce, substitute 1 tablespoon tomato sauce mixed with 1 tablespoon adobo sauce with chipotles.*

1. Preheat oven to 325°F. Grease 9-inch square baking pan. Arrange 3 to 4 bread slices to cover bottom of pan; cut bread to fit, if necessary. Spread chipotle sauce over bread. Layer turkey over sauce. Sprinkle 1 cup cheese over turkey. Cover with remaining bread slices.

2. Whisk milk, eggs, salt and pepper in medium bowl until blended. Pour over bread, and press down firmly so bread absorbs liquid. Top with remaining $\frac{1}{2}$ cup cheese.

3. Bake for 60 to 70 minutes or until eggs are set and golden brown. Remove from oven; let stand 10 to 15 minutes before slicing.

*Makes 6 servings*

# Aunt Marilyn's Cinnamon French Toast Casserole

1 large loaf French bread, cut into 1$\frac{1}{2}$-inch slices
3$\frac{1}{2}$ cups milk
9 eggs
1$\frac{1}{2}$ cups granulated sugar, divided
1 tablespoon vanilla
$\frac{1}{2}$ teaspoon salt
6 to 8 medium baking apples, such as McIntosh or Cortland, peeled and sliced
1 teaspoon ground cinnamon
$\frac{1}{2}$ teaspoon ground nutmeg
Powdered sugar (optional)

1. Place bread slices in greased 13×9-inch glass baking dish or casserole.

2. Whisk milk, eggs, 1 cup granulated sugar, vanilla and salt in large bowl until well blended. Pour half of mixture over bread.

3. Layer apple slices over bread. Pour remaining egg mixture over apples.

4. Combine remaining $\frac{1}{2}$ cup granulated sugar, cinnamon and nutmeg in small bowl; sprinkle over casserole. Cover and refrigerate overnight.

5. Preheat oven to 350°F. Bake, uncovered, 1 hour or until eggs are set. Sprinkle with powdered sugar. *Makes 6 to 8 servings*

# Biscuit and Sausage Bake

2 cups biscuit baking mix
½ cup milk
1 egg
1 teaspoon vanilla
1 cup fresh or frozen blueberries
6 fully cooked breakfast sausage links, thawed if frozen, cut
   into small pieces
Maple syrup, warmed

1. Preheat oven to 350°F. Spray 8-inch square baking pan with nonstick cooking spray.

2. Whisk baking mix, milk, egg and vanilla in medium bowl. Stir in blueberries. (Batter will be stiff.) Spread batter into prepared pan. Sprinkle sausage pieces over batter.

3. Bake 22 minutes or until lightly browned on top. Cut into squares; serve with maple syrup. *Makes 6 servings*

Prep Time: **10 minutes**
Bake Time: **22 minutes**

Since blueberries have such a short season, freeze some during the summer so that you can bake with them all year long. Spread unwashed berries in a single layer on a baking sheet. Freeze 2 hours and remove berries to a food storage bag and keep in the freezer. Just rinse and drain berries when ready to use.

# Monterey Chicken and Rice Quiche

4 boneless skinless chicken tenderloins, cut into 1-inch pieces
1$\frac{3}{4}$ cups water
  1 box UNCLE BEN'S® COUNTRY INN® Chicken & Vegetable Rice
  1 cup frozen mixed vegetables
  1 (9-inch) deep-dish ready-to-use frozen pie crust
  3 eggs
  $\frac{1}{2}$ cup milk
  $\frac{1}{2}$ cup (2 ounces) shredded Monterey Jack cheese

1. Heat oven to 400°F.

2. In large skillet, combine chicken, water, rice, contents of seasoning packet and frozen vegetables. Bring to a boil. Cover; reduce heat and simmer 10 minutes. Spoon mixture into pie crust.

3. In small bowl, beat eggs and milk. Pour over rice mixture in pie crust; top with cheese. Bake 30 to 35 minutes or until knife inserted in center comes out clean. *Makes 6 servings*

Serving Suggestion: A fresh fruit compote of orange sections and green grapes or blueberries is the perfect accompaniment to this delicious quiche.

# Sunny Day Casserole

1 jar (8 ounces) pasteurized processed cheese spread, melted
3/4 cup milk
4 cups diced potatoes, partially cooked
2 cups diced **HILLSHIRE FARM**® Ham
1 package (16 ounces) frozen mixed vegetables, thawed
1/2 cup chopped onion
1 cup (4 ounces) shredded Swiss, Cheddar or Monterey Jack cheese
1 cup cracker crumbs

Preheat oven to 350°F.

Combine cheese spread and milk in large bowl. Stir in potatoes, Ham, mixed vegetables and onion. Pour into medium casserole. Bake, covered, 45 minutes, stirring occasionally. Sprinkle cheese and cracker crumbs over top. Bake, uncovered, until cheese is melted.          *Makes 6 servings*

# SPAM™ Breakfast Burritos

1 (12-ounce) can **SPAM**® Classic, cubed
4 eggs
2 tablespoons milk
1 tablespoon butter or margarine
1 cup (4 ounces) shredded Cheddar cheese, divided
1 cup (4 ounces) shredded Monterey Jack cheese, divided
6 (6-inch) **MANNY'S**® Soft Taco Flour Tortillas
   **CHI-CHI'S**® Salsa

Heat oven to 400°F. In medium bowl, beat together SPAM®, eggs and milk. Melt butter in large skillet; add egg mixture. Cook, stirring, to desired doneness. Divide SPAM™ mixture and half of cheeses evenly among tortillas. Roll up tortillas; place seam side down in 12×8-inch baking dish. Sprinkle remaining cheeses over top of burritos. Bake 5 to 10 minutes or until cheese is melted. Serve with CHI-CHI'S® Salsa.          *Makes 6 servings*

# Bacon and Maple Grits Puff

8 slices bacon
2 cups milk
1 1/4 cups water
1 cup uncooked quick-cooking grits
1/2 teaspoon salt
1/2 cup pure maple syrup
4 eggs
Fresh chives (optional)

1. Preheat oven to 350°F. Grease 1 1/2-quart round casserole or soufflé dish; set aside.

2. Cook bacon in large skillet over medium-high heat about 7 minutes or until crisp. Drain on paper towels. Reserve 2 tablespoons bacon drippings.

3. Combine milk, water, grits and salt in medium saucepan. Bring to a boil over medium heat, stirring frequently. Reduce heat; simmer 2 to 3 minutes or until mixture thickens, stirring constantly. Remove from heat; stir in syrup and reserved 2 tablespoons bacon drippings.

4. Crumble bacon; reserve 1/4 cup for garnish. Stir remaining crumbled bacon into grits mixture.

5. Beat eggs in medium bowl with electric mixer at high speed until thick and pale. Stir spoonful of grits mixture into eggs until well blended. Fold egg mixture into remaining grits mixture until blended. Pour grits mixture into prepared casserole.

6. Bake 1 hour 20 minutes or until knife inserted into center comes out clean. Top with reserved bacon and chives. Serve immediately.

*Makes 6 to 8 servings*

Note: Puff will fall slightly after being removed from oven.

# Fruited Corn Pudding

5 cups frozen corn, thawed, divided
5 eggs
$\frac{1}{2}$ cup milk
$1\frac{1}{2}$ cups whipping cream
$\frac{1}{3}$ cup unsalted butter, melted and cooled
1 teaspoon vanilla
$\frac{1}{2}$ teaspoon salt
$\frac{1}{4}$ teaspoon ground nutmeg
3 tablespoons dried cranberries or raisins
3 tablespoons finely chopped dried apricots
3 tablespoons finely chopped dates
2 tablespoons finely chopped dried pears or other dried fruit

1. Preheat oven to 350°F. Grease 13×9-inch baking dish; set aside.

2. Combine $3\frac{1}{2}$ cups corn, eggs and milk in food processor; cover and process until mixture is almost smooth.

3. Transfer corn mixture to large bowl. Add cream, butter, vanilla, salt and nutmeg; stir until well blended. Stir in remaining $1\frac{1}{2}$ cups corn, cranberries, apricots, dates and pears. Spoon mixture into prepared dish.

4. Bake 50 to 60 minutes or until pudding is set and top begins to brown. Let stand 10 to 15 minutes before serving.     *Makes 8 to 10 servings*

# Crustless Southwestern Quiche

8 ounces chorizo sausage,* casings removed

8 eggs

1 package (10 ounces) frozen chopped spinach, thawed and
   squeezed dry

1 cup (4 ounces) crumbled queso fresco or 1 cup (4 ounces) shredded
   Cheddar cheese

$\frac{1}{2}$ cup whipping cream or half-and-half

$\frac{1}{4}$ cup salsa

*Chorizo, a spicy Mexican pork sausage, is flavored with garlic and chiles. It is
available in most supermarkets. If it is not available, substitute 8 ounces bulk pork
sausage plus $\frac{1}{4}$ teaspoon ground red pepper.

1. Preheat oven to 400°F. Grease 10-inch quiche dish or deep-dish pie
plate.

2. Brown sausage in medium skillet over medium heat, stirring to break up
meat; drain fat. Cool 5 minutes.

3. Beat eggs in medium bowl. Add spinach, sausage, cheese and cream;
mix well. Pour into prepared quiche dish. Bake 20 minutes or until center is
set. Let stand 5 minutes before cutting into wedges. Serve with salsa.

*Makes 4 servings*

# Ham and Egg Enchiladas

2 tablespoons butter
1 small red bell pepper, chopped
3 green onions, sliced
$\frac{1}{2}$ cup diced ham
8 eggs
8 (7- to 8-inch) flour tortillas
$\frac{1}{2}$ cup (2 ounces) pepper jack cheese
1 can (10 ounces) enchilada sauce
$\frac{1}{2}$ cup salsa
$1\frac{1}{2}$ cups (6 ounces) pepper jack cheese (optional)

1. Preheat oven to 350°F.

2. Melt butter in large nonstick skillet over medium heat. Add bell pepper and onions; cook and stir 2 minutes. Add ham; cook and stir 1 minute.

3. Lightly beat eggs with wire whisk in medium bowl. Add eggs to skillet; cook until eggs are set but still soft, stirring occasionally.

4. Spoon about $\frac{1}{3}$ cup egg mixture evenly down center of each tortilla; top with 1 tablespoon cheese. Roll up tortillas and place seam side down in shallow 11×7-inch baking dish.

5. Combine enchilada sauce and salsa in small bowl; pour evenly over enchiladas.

6. Cover dish with foil; bake 20 minutes. Uncover; sprinkle with $1\frac{1}{2}$ cups cheese, if desired. Continue baking 10 minutes or until enchiladas are heated through and cheese is melted.          *Makes 4 servings*

# Spicy Sausage Popover Pizza

 $^1/_2$ **pound turkey breakfast sausage patties**
 $^1/_2$ **pound 93% lean ground turkey**
 $^1/_3$ **cup chopped onion**
  1 **clove garlic, minced**
 $^3/_4$ **cup chopped red bell pepper**
1$^1/_2$ **cups all-purpose flour**
 $^1/_4$ **teaspoon salt**
 $^1/_4$ **teaspoon red pepper flakes**
  1 **cup milk**
  3 **eggs** *or* $^3/_4$ **cup cholesterol-free egg substitute**
  1 **cup (4 ounces) shredded Cheddar cheese**
 $^1/_2$ **cup (2 ounces) shredded mozzarella cheese**
 $^1/_2$ **cup prepared pizza sauce**

1. Preheat oven to 425°F. Generously spray 13×9-inch baking dish with nonstick cooking spray; set aside.

2. Crumble turkey sausage patties in large skillet; add ground turkey, onion and garlic. Cook over medium heat until turkey is no longer pink; drain fat. Stir in bell pepper; set aside.

3. Combine flour, salt and red pepper flakes in medium bowl. Combine milk and eggs in another medium bowl; whisk into flour mixture until smooth. Pour into prepared baking dish; sprinkle with sausage mixture. Sprinkle with cheeses. Bake, uncovered, 21 to 23 minutes or until puffed and golden brown.

4. Microwave pizza sauce on HIGH 1 minute. Serve with sauce.

*Makes 8 servings*

Prep Time: **15 minutes**
Bake Time: **21 to 23 minutes**

# Breakfast Casserole

6 large eggs, beaten
$\frac{1}{2}$ cup sour cream
1 can (15 ounces) VEG•ALL® Original Mixed Vegetables, drained
1 cup frozen cubed hash brown potatoes, thawed
1 cup smoked sausage links, chopped
1 cup shredded pepper-jack cheese
2 tablespoons canned jalapeño pepper slices
1 cup broken tortilla chips

Preheat oven to 350°F.

In medium bowl, combine eggs and sour cream until smooth. Fold in remaining ingredients except tortilla chips.

Transfer mixture to greased 11×7-inch baking dish. Bake for 25 to 30 minutes or until eggs are set and puffed.

Top with tortilla chips and bake an additional 5 minutes. Serve with additional sour cream on the side, if desired.

Serve with fresh fruit for breakfast or brunch.          *Makes 6 to 8 servings*

Variation: For a milder flavor, substitute chopped fresh cilantro for the sliced jalapeño peppers.

# Spinach Sensation

$^1/_2$ pound sliced bacon

1 cup (8 ounces) sour cream

3 eggs, separated

2 tablespoons all-purpose flour

$^1/_8$ teaspoon black pepper

1 package (10 ounces) frozen chopped spinach, thawed and
squeezed dry

$^1/_2$ cup (2 ounces) shredded sharp Cheddar cheese

$^1/_2$ cup dry bread crumbs

1 tablespoon butter, melted

1. Preheat oven to 350°F. Spray 2-quart round baking dish with nonstick cooking spray.

2. Place bacon in single layer in large skillet; cook over medium heat until crisp. Remove from skillet; drain on paper towels. Crumble and set aside.

3. Combine sour cream, egg yolks, flour and pepper in large bowl; set aside. Beat egg whites in medium bowl with electric mixer at high speed until stiff peaks form. Stir one-fourth whipped egg whites into sour cream mixture; fold in remaining egg whites.

4. Arrange half of spinach in prepared dish. Top with half of sour cream mixture; sprinkle with $^1/_4$ cup cheese. Sprinkle bacon over cheese. Repeat layers, ending with $^1/_4$ cup cheese.

5. Combine bread crumbs and butter in small bowl; sprinkle evenly over cheese. Bake, uncovered, 30 to 35 minutes or until eggs are set. Let stand 5 minutes before serving. *Makes 6 servings*

# Buon Giorno Frittata

4 eggs, beaten
2 egg whites, beaten
$\frac{1}{4}$ cup shredded fresh basil
2 tablespoons low-fat milk
$\frac{1}{4}$ teaspoon salt
$\frac{1}{8}$ teaspoon black pepper
2 teaspoons olive oil
2 cups halved and sliced zucchini
1 cup diced yellow onions
1 can (6 ounces) California Ripe Olives, drained and halved
$\frac{1}{2}$ cup roasted red bell peppers, sliced into $\frac{1}{4}$-inch strips
$\frac{1}{4}$ cup grated fontina or Parmesan cheese

1. Preheat oven to 400°F. In a medium-sized mixing bowl, whisk together eggs, egg whites, basil, milk, salt and pepper. Set aside

2. Heat oil in a 10-inch oven-proof skillet over medium heat. Add zucchini and onions and cook for 5 to 6 minutes or until tender. Mix in 1 cup of California Ripe Olives and red bell peppers. Remove from heat and stir into egg mixture.

3. Pour egg and vegetable mixture back into pan. Turn heat to medium-high and cook for 3 to 5 minutes until eggs are set on the bottom. Sprinkle the top of the frittata with grated cheese and remaining California Ripe Olives. Place frittata in oven for 13 to 15 minutes or until cooked through.

4. Cool slightly and cut into 6 wedges.                    *Makes 6 servings*

Serving Suggestion: **Serve with crusty country bread.**

Favorite recipe from **California Olive Industry**

# Cheddar and Leek Strata

8 eggs, lightly beaten
2 cups milk
$\frac{1}{2}$ cup porter ale or beer
2 cloves garlic, minced
$\frac{1}{4}$ teaspoon salt
$\frac{1}{4}$ teaspoon black pepper
1 loaf (16 ounces) sourdough bread, cut into $\frac{1}{2}$-inch cubes
2 small leeks, coarsely chopped
1 red bell pepper, chopped
$1\frac{1}{2}$ cups (6 ounces) shredded Swiss cheese
$1\frac{1}{2}$ cups (6 ounces) shredded sharp Cheddar cheese
    Fresh sage sprigs (optional)

1. Beat eggs, milk, ale, garlic, salt and black pepper in large bowl until well blended.

2. Spread half of bread cubes on bottom of greased 13×9-inch baking dish. Sprinkle half of leeks and half of bell pepper over bread cubes. Top with $\frac{3}{4}$ cup Swiss cheese and $\frac{3}{4}$ cup Cheddar cheese. Repeat layers.

3. Pour egg mixture evenly over top. Cover tightly with plastic wrap or foil. Weigh top of strata down with slightly smaller baking dish. Refrigerate strata at least 2 hours or overnight.

4. Preheat oven to 350°F. Bake, uncovered, 40 to 45 minutes or until center is set. Garnish as desired. *Makes 12 servings*

# Ham and Cheese Bread Pudding

1 small loaf (8 ounces) sourdough, French or Italian bread, cut into
   1-inch-thick slices
3 tablespoons butter or margarine, softened
8 ounces ham or smoked ham, cubed
2 cups (8 ounces) shredded Cheddar cheese
3 eggs
2 cups milk
1 teaspoon dry mustard
$\frac{1}{2}$ teaspoon salt
$\frac{1}{8}$ teaspoon white pepper

1. Grease 11×7-inch baking dish. Spread 1 side of each bread slice with butter. Cut into 1-inch cubes; place on bottom of prepared dish. Top with ham; sprinkle with cheese.

2. Beat eggs in medium bowl. Whisk in milk, mustard, salt and pepper. Pour egg mixture evenly in dish. Cover; refrigerate at least 6 hours or overnight.

3. Preheat oven to 350°F. Bake bread pudding, uncovered, 45 to 50 minutes or until puffed and golden brown and knife inserted into center comes out clean. Garnish as desired.                    *Makes 8 servings*

# Chile-Corn Quiche

1 (9-inch) deep-dish pastry shell
1 can (8¾ ounces) whole kernel corn, drained, *or* 1 cup frozen whole
    kernel corn, thawed
1 can (4 ounces) diced mild green chiles, drained
¼ cup thinly sliced green onions
1 cup (4 ounces) shredded Monterey Jack cheese
3 eggs
1½ cups half-and-half
½ teaspoon salt
½ teaspoon ground cumin

1. Preheat oven to 450°F. Place pastry shell in 9-inch deep dish pie plate. Line with foil; partially fill with uncooked beans or rice to weight shell. Bake 10 minutes. Remove foil and beans; continue baking pastry 5 minutes or until lightly browned. Let cool. *Reduce oven temperature to 375°F.*

2. Combine corn, green chiles and green onions in small bowl. Spoon into pastry shell; sprinkle with cheese. Whisk eggs, half-and-half, salt and cumin in medium bowl. Pour over cheese.

3. Bake 35 to 45 minutes or until filling is puffed and knife inserted into center comes out clean. Let stand 10 minutes before serving.

*Makes 6 servings*

# Ham 'n' Apple Breakfast Casserole Slices

**1 package (15 ounces) refrigerated pie crusts (2 crusts)**
**20 pieces (about 1 pound) thinly sliced ham, cut into bite-size pieces**
**1 can (21 ounces) apple pie filling**
**1 cup (4 ounces) shredded sharp Cheddar cheese**
**¼ cup plus 1 teaspoon sugar, divided**
**½ teaspoon ground cinnamon**

1. Preheat oven to 425°F.

2. Place one crust in 9-inch pie pan, allowing edges to hang over sides. Arrange half of ham pieces on bottom crust. Spoon apple filling onto ham. Arrange remaining ham on top of apples; sprinkle with cheese.

3. Mix ¼ cup sugar and cinnamon in small bowl; sprinkle evenly over cheese. Arrange second crust over filling and crimp edges together. Brush crust lightly with water and sprinkle with remaining 1 teaspoon sugar. Cut slits for steam to escape.

4. Bake 20 to 25 minutes or until crust is golden brown. Cool 15 minutes before slicing. *Makes 6 servings*

 *Tip*

Refrigerated pie crusts are a great product to keep on hand for quick dishes. They can be used for savory items, like quiches, or for sweet pies and desserts.

# Hash Brown Breakfast Casserole

3 cups frozen shredded hash brown potatoes, thawed
1$\frac{1}{2}$ cups (6 ounces) finely chopped ham
$\frac{3}{4}$ cup (3 ounces) shredded Cheddar cheese
$\frac{1}{4}$ cup sliced green onions
1 can (12 ounces) evaporated milk
1 tablespoon all-purpose flour
4 eggs *or* 1 cup cholesterol-free egg substitute
$\frac{1}{2}$ teaspoon black pepper

1. Lightly coat 8-inch square baking dish with nonstick cooking spray.

2. Layer potatoes, ham, cheese and green onions in prepared dish. Whisk milk and flour in small bowl. Stir in eggs and pepper; pour evenly over casserole. Cover and refrigerate 4 hours or overnight.

3. Preheat oven to 350°F. Bake, uncovered, 55 to 60 minutes or until knife inserted into center comes out clean. Remove from oven; let stand 10 minutes before serving.                    *Makes 6 servings*

Prep Time: **10 minutes**
Chill Time: **4 hours**
Bake Time: **55 minutes**

# Meatless
## *Main Dishes*

# Luscious Vegetarian Lasagna

8 ounces lasagna noodles

1 can (about 14 ounces) whole peeled tomatoes, undrained and chopped

1 can (12 ounces) tomato sauce

1 teaspoon dried oregano

1 teaspoon dried basil

Dash black pepper

2 tablespoons olive oil

1 large onion, chopped

1½ teaspoons minced garlic

2 small zucchini, diced

1 large carrot, diced

1 green bell pepper, diced

8 ounces mushrooms, sliced

2 cups cottage cheese

1 cup (4 ounces) shredded mozzarella cheese

1 cup grated Parmesan or Romano cheese

Parsley sprigs (optional)

1. Cook noodles according to package directions; drain.

2. Combine tomatoes with juice, tomato sauce, oregano, basil and black pepper in large saucepan; bring to a boil over high heat. Reduce heat; simmer, uncovered, 6 to 10 minutes.

3. Heat oil in large skillet over medium-high heat. Add onion and garlic; cook and stir 5 minutes or until onion is golden. Add zucchini, carrot, bell pepper and mushrooms. Cook and stir 5 to 10 minutes or until vegetables are tender. Stir vegetables into tomato mixture; bring to a boil. Reduce heat; simmer, uncovered, 15 minutes.

4. Preheat oven to 350°F. Combine cheeses in large bowl; blend well.

5. Spoon about 1 cup sauce in bottom of 13×9-inch baking pan. Place half

of noodles over sauce, then half of cheese mixture and half of remaining sauce. Repeat layers.

6. Bake lasagna 30 to 45 minutes or until bubbly. Let stand 10 minutes. Garnish with parsley.                                    *Makes 6 to 8 servings*

## Cranberry Wild Rice Casserole

    1 box (6.7 ounces) brown and wild rice mix (mushroom recipe)
    1 cup cooked chicken, cubed
$1/4$ cup Marsala wine (optional)
$1/2$ cup dried cranberries
$3/4$ cup chopped walnuts
    1 tablespoon grated orange zest
$2^{1}/2$ cups water
    1 tablespoon butter
    1 can (15 ounces) VEG•ALL® Original Mixed Vegetables, drained
       Salt & pepper to taste
$1/3$ cup goat cheese, crumbled, optional

Combine the first eight ingredients in a 2-quart casserole dish.

Cover and microwave on high for 10 minutes.

Stir in Veg•All, cover and microwave an additional 10 to 15 minutes or until rice is cooked and liquid is absorbed. Season to taste with salt and pepper.

Garnish with orange zest and fresh parsley.                                    *Makes 5 cups*

Cook's note: Cover and let stand for 5 minutes. Sprinkle with goat cheese if desired.

Meatless Main Dishes

# Zucornchile Rajas Bake

2 cups tomato sauce
2 tablespoons chili powder
2 tablespoons tomato paste
1 tablespoon cider vinegar
1 teaspoon ground cumin
$\frac{1}{2}$ teaspoon salt
$\frac{1}{2}$ teaspoon garlic powder
$\frac{1}{4}$ teaspoon ground red pepper
6 corn tortillas
   Vegetable oil for frying
1 pound zucchini, thinly sliced (about 3 cups)
$1\frac{1}{2}$ cups (6 ounces) shredded Monterey Jack cheese, divided
1 cup corn
1 can (4 ounces) diced green chiles, drained
$\frac{1}{2}$ to 1 cup sour cream
3 green onions, chopped

1. Preheat oven to 350°F. Grease 13×9-inch baking dish.

2. Combine tomato sauce, chili powder, tomato paste, vinegar, cumin, salt, garlic powder and red pepper in medium saucepan; bring to a boil over high heat. Reduce heat; simmer 10 minutes, stirring occasionally.

3. Meanwhile, cut tortillas into $\frac{1}{4}$-inch-wide strips. Heat enough oil to cover bottom of medium skillet by $\frac{1}{2}$ inch. Fry tortilla strips in batches until crisp; drain on paper towels.

4. Steam zucchini 5 minutes; drain. Transfer to large bowl. Add $\frac{3}{4}$ cup cheese, corn, chiles and half of tortilla strips. Toss lightly to combine; spoon into prepared baking dish. Spread tomato sauce mixture over zucchini mixture and top with remaining $\frac{3}{4}$ cup cheese. Bake 30 minutes or until heated through. Serve with remaining tortilla strips, sour cream and green onions. *Makes 6 to 8 servings*

# Spinach and Mushroom Enchiladas

2 packages (10 ounces each) frozen chopped spinach, thawed

1$\frac{1}{2}$ cups sliced mushrooms

1 can (about 15 ounces) pinto beans, rinsed and drained

3 teaspoons chili powder, divided

$\frac{1}{4}$ teaspoon red pepper flakes

1 can (8 ounces) tomato sauce

2 tablespoons water

$\frac{1}{2}$ teaspoon hot pepper sauce

8 (8-inch) corn tortillas

1 cup (4 ounces) shredded Monterey Jack cheese

Shredded lettuce

Chopped tomatoes

Sour cream

Chopped cilantro

1. Combine spinach, mushrooms, beans, 2 teaspoons chili powder and red pepper flakes in large skillet over medium heat. Cook and stir 5 minutes; remove from heat.

2. Combine tomato sauce, water, remaining 1 teaspoon chili powder and pepper sauce in medium skillet. Dip tortillas into tomato sauce mixture; stack tortillas on waxed paper.

3. Divide spinach filling into 8 portions. Spoon down center of tortillas; roll up and place seam side down in 11×7-inch microwavable dish. Spread remaining tomato sauce mixture over enchiladas.

4. Cover with vented plastic wrap. Microwave, uncovered, on MEDIUM (50%) 10 minutes or until heated through. Sprinkle with cheese. Microwave on MEDIUM 3 minutes or until cheese is melted. Serve with lettuce, tomatoes, sour cream and cilantro. *Makes 4 servings*

# Ragú® No-Boiling Lasagna

2 containers (15 ounces each) ricotta cheese
2 cups shredded mozzarella cheese (about 8 ounces)
$\frac{1}{2}$ cup grated Parmesan cheese
2 eggs
2 jars (1 pound 10 ounces each) RAGÚ® Old World Style® Pasta Sauce
12 uncooked lasagna noodles

1. Preheat oven to 375°F. In bowl, combine ricotta, 1 cup mozzarella, $\frac{1}{4}$ cup Parmesan cheese and eggs.

2. In 13×9-inch baking dish, spread 1 cup Ragú Pasta Sauce. Layer 4 uncooked noodles, then 1 cup sauce and $\frac{1}{2}$ of the ricotta mixture; repeat. Top with remaining 4 uncooked noodles and 2 cups sauce. Cover tightly with aluminum foil and bake 1 hour.

3. Remove foil and sprinkle with remaining cheeses. Bake uncovered an additional 10 minutes. Let stand 10 minutes before serving. Serve with remaining sauce, heated.                      *Makes 12 servings*

Variation: For a twist on a classic, add 1 pound ground beef, cooked, to pasta sauce.

Note: Recipe can be halved. Bake in an 11×7-inch baking dish 1 hour. Continue as above, omitting last 10 minutes of baking.

Prep Time: 10 minutes
Cook Time: 70 minutes

# Fabulous Feta Frittata

2 tablespoons butter or olive oil
8 eggs
$\frac{1}{4}$ cup half-and-half
$\frac{1}{4}$ cup chopped fresh basil
$\frac{1}{2}$ teaspoon salt
$\frac{1}{4}$ teaspoon black pepper
1 package (4 ounces) crumbled feta cheese with basil, olives and sun-dried tomatoes *or* 1 cup crumbled feta cheese
$\frac{1}{4}$ cup pine nuts

1. Preheat broiler. Melt butter in 10-inch broilerproof skillet over medium heat. Tilt skillet so bottom and side are well coated with butter. Beat eggs, half-and-half, basil, salt and pepper in large bowl until well blended. Pour mixture into skillet. Cover; cook 8 to 10 minutes or until eggs are set around edge (center will be wet).

2. Sprinkle cheese and pine nuts evenly over frittata. Transfer to broiler; broil 2 minutes or until center of frittata is set and pine nuts are golden brown. *Makes 4 servings*

# Barley Vegetable Casserole

**Nonstick cooking spray**
**$^2/_3$ cup uncooked barley (not quick-cooking)**
**$2^1/_4$ cups vegetable broth, divided**
**4 cups frozen mixed vegetables (including broccoli, cauliflower, carrots and onions), thawed and drained**
**1 teaspoon garlic powder**
**$^1/_2$ teaspoon black pepper**
**1 tablespoon butter**
**$^1/_2$ teaspoon salt**

1. Preheat oven to 350°F. Coat 1-quart casserole with cooking spray.

2. Place barley and $^1/_4$ cup vegetable broth in nonstick skillet; cook over medium heat 3 minutes or until lightly browned, stirring frequently. Transfer to prepared casserole.

3. Add vegetables, garlic powder, pepper and remaining 2 cups broth to casserole; mix well.

4. Cover and bake 50 minutes or until barley is tender and most of liquid is absorbed. Stir several times during baking. Stir in butter and salt.

*Makes 4 servings*

# Bowtie Zucchini

1/4 cup vegetable oil
1 cup chopped onion
2 cloves garlic, minced
5 small zucchini, cut into thin strips
2/3 cup whipping cream
1 package (16 ounces) bowtie pasta, cooked and drained
3 tablespoons grated Parmesan cheese
Salt and black pepper

1. Preheat oven to 350°F.

2. Heat oil in large skillet over medium-high heat. Add onion and garlic; cook and stir until onion is tender. Add zucchini; cook and stir until tender.

3. Add cream; cook and stir until thickened. Add pasta and cheese to skillet. Season to taste with salt and pepper. Transfer mixture to 2-quart casserole. Cover and bake 15 minutes or until heated through.

*Makes 8 servings*

# Broccoli Lasagna

2 tablespoons olive oil

1 cup thinly sliced fresh mushrooms

3 cloves garlic, chopped

1 can (about 14 ounces) diced tomatoes

1 can (8 ounces) tomato sauce

1 can (6 ounces) tomato paste

1 tablespoon red wine vinegar

1 teaspoon dried oregano *or* 1 tablespoon fresh oregano, chopped

1 teaspoon dried basil *or* 1 tablespoon fresh basil, chopped

Pinch red pepper flakes

2 cups ricotta cheese

1 cup mozzarella cheese, divided

1/4 cup chopped fresh parsley

9 lasagna noodles, cooked and well drained

3 cups chopped broccoli (about 1 large bunch), cooked and well drained

1 to 2 tablespoons grated Parmesan cheese

1. Preheat oven to 350°F. Spray 8-inch square pan with cooking spray. Combine ricotta, mozzarella and parsley in medium bowl; set aside.

2. Heat oil in large saucepan over medium heat. Add mushrooms and garlic; cook and stir about 5 minutes or until mushrooms are browned and beginning to release liquid. Stir in tomatoes, tomato sauce, tomato paste, vinegar, oregano, basil and red pepper flakes; simmer, stirring occasionally.

3. Place 3 lasagna noodles in bottom of prepared pan. Spread half of ricotta mixture over noodles. Layer half of broccoli over ricotta mixture. Spoon about one-third tomato mixture over broccoli. Repeat layers.

4. Cover with foil; bake 25 minutes. Uncover; sprinkle with remaining mozzarella and Parmesan cheeses. Bake, uncovered, 10 minutes or until cheese is melted. Let stand 10 minutes before serving.

*Makes 4 to 6 servings*

# Cheesy Baked Barley

  2 cups water
 $\frac{1}{2}$ cup medium uncooked pearl barley
 $\frac{1}{2}$ teaspoon salt, divided
    Nonstick cooking spray
 $\frac{1}{2}$ cup diced onion
 $\frac{1}{2}$ cup diced zucchini
 $\frac{1}{2}$ cup diced red bell pepper
1$\frac{1}{2}$ teaspoons all-purpose flour
 $\frac{3}{4}$ cup milk
  1 cup (4 ounces) shredded Italian cheese blend, divided
  1 tablespoon Dijon mustard
    Salt and black pepper

1. Bring water to a boil in small saucepan. Add barley and $\frac{1}{4}$ teaspoon salt. Reduce heat; cover and simmer 45 minutes or until barley is tender and water is absorbed. Remove from heat. Let stand, covered, 5 minutes.

2. Preheat oven to 375°F. Spray medium skillet with cooking spray. Cook onion, zucchini and bell pepper over medium-low heat about 10 minutes or until tender. Stir in flour and remaining $\frac{1}{4}$ teaspoon salt; cook 1 to 2 minutes. Add milk, stirring constantly; cook and stir until slightly thickened. Remove from heat. Add barley, $\frac{3}{4}$ cup cheese and mustard; stir until cheese is melted. Season with salt and black pepper.

3. Spread evenly in 1-quart casserole. Sprinkle with remaining $\frac{1}{4}$ cup cheese. Bake 20 minutes or until heated through and cheese is lightly browned. *Makes 2 servings*

# Pasta & White Bean Casserole

1 tablespoon olive oil
$\frac{1}{2}$ cup chopped onion
2 cloves garlic, minced
2 cans (about 15 ounces each) cannellini beans, rinsed and drained
3 cups cooked small shell pasta
1 can (8 ounces) tomato sauce
$1\frac{1}{2}$ teaspoons Italian seasoning
$\frac{1}{2}$ teaspoon salt
$\frac{1}{2}$ teaspoon black pepper
1 cup (4 ounces) shredded Italian cheese blend
2 tablespoons finely chopped fresh parsley

1. Preheat oven to 350°F. Spray 2-quart casserole with nonstick cooking spray.

2. Heat oil in large skillet over medium-high heat. Add onion and garlic; cook and stir 3 to 4 minutes or until onion is tender.

3. Add beans, pasta, tomato sauce, Italian seasoning, salt and pepper; mix well.

4. Transfer to prepared casserole; sprinkle with cheese and parsley. Bake 20 minutes or until cheese is melted. *Makes 6 servings*

# My Mac & Cheese

$\frac{1}{4}$ cup ($\frac{1}{2}$ stick) butter
$\frac{1}{4}$ cup all-purpose flour
 2 cups milk
$\frac{1}{2}$ pound sharp Cheddar cheese, cut into $\frac{1}{2}$-inch cubes
 8 slices (about 2 ounces) pepper jack cheese, cut into pieces
    (optional)
$\frac{1}{2}$ cup chopped onion
 2 cups (about 16 ounces) broccoli florets, steamed until tender
 2 cups macaroni, cooked and drained
 2 English muffins, cut into $\frac{1}{2}$-inch pieces

1. Preheat oven to 350°F.

2. Melt butter in large saucepan over medium heat. Stir in flour to make smooth paste; cook and stir 2 minutes. Gradually add milk, stirring constantly, until mixture is slightly thickened.

3. Add Cheddar cheese, pepper jack cheese, if desired, and onion to milk mixture. Cook, stirring constantly, until cheese is melted. Add broccoli; mix well.

4. Place macaroni in 3-quart casserole. Add cheese mixture; mix well. Sprinkle English muffin pieces evenly over top. Bake 15 to 20 minutes or until muffin pieces are golden brown.          *Makes 4 to 6 servings*

# Barley and Swiss Chard Skillet Casserole

1 cup water
1 cup chopped red bell pepper
1 cup chopped green bell pepper
$^3/_4$ cup uncooked quick-cooking barley
$^1/_8$ teaspoon garlic powder
$^1/_8$ teaspoon red pepper flakes
2 cups coarsely chopped packed Swiss chard leaves*
1 cup canned navy beans, rinsed and drained
1 cup quartered grape tomatoes
$^1/_4$ cup chopped fresh basil leaves
1 tablespoon olive oil
2 tablespoons Italian-seasoned dry bread crumbs

*Fresh spinach or beet greens can be substituted for Swiss chard.

1. Preheat broiler.

2. Bring water to a boil in large skillet; add bell peppers, barley, garlic powder and red pepper flakes. Reduce heat; cover and simmer 10 minutes or until liquid is absorbed.

3. Remove skillet from heat. Stir in chard, beans, tomatoes, basil and olive oil. Sprinkle evenly with bread crumbs. Broil, uncovered, 2 minutes or until golden brown. *Makes 4 servings*

# Roasted Vegetable Salad with Capers and Walnuts

**Salad**

   1 pound small Brussels sprouts
   1 pound very small Yukon Gold potatoes
   $1/4$ teaspoon salt
   $1/4$ teaspoon dried rosemary
   $1/4$ teaspoon black pepper
   3 tablespoons olive oil
   1 large red bell pepper, cut into bite-size chunks
   $1/4$ cup walnuts, coarsely chopped
   2 tablespoons capers

**Dressing**

   $1^1/_2$ tablespoons white wine vinegar
   2 tablespoons extra-virgin olive oil
   Salt and black pepper to taste

1. Preheat oven to 400°F. For salad, wash, trim and pat dry Brussels sprouts. Slash bottoms. Scrub and pat dry potatoes; cut into halves.

2. Place Brussels sprouts and potatoes in shallow roasting pan; sprinkle with salt, rosemary and pepper. Drizzle with olive oil; toss to coat. Roast 20 minutes. Stir in bell pepper; roast 15 minutes or until vegetables are tender. Transfer to large serving bowl; stir in walnuts and capers.

3. For dressing, whisk vinegar, oil, salt and pepper in small bowl until well blended. Pour over salad; toss to coat. Serve at room temperature.

*Makes 2 servings*

Potluck Tip: To bring Roast Vegetable Salad as a potluck dish, prepare in advance. Cover and refrigerate up to one day. Serve at room temperature at your host's home.

# Tamale Potato Quiche

$\frac{1}{2}$ pound small red potatoes, peeled and sliced $\frac{1}{8}$ inch thick
1 cup white cornmeal
1 teaspoon ground cumin
$\frac{3}{4}$ teaspoon salt, divided
2 cups (8 ounces) shredded Cheddar cheese, divided
4 eggs, divided
$\frac{1}{3}$ cup water
2 tablespoons olive oil
$\frac{1}{2}$ cup cottage cheese
2 tablespoons milk
$\frac{1}{4}$ teaspoon black pepper
1 can (4 ounces) chopped green chiles, drained
1 medium red bell pepper, seeded and cut into thin strips

1. Place potatoes in small saucepan; cover with water. Bring to a boil over high heat. Reduce heat; cover and simmer 5 minutes or until potatoes are crisp-tender. Drain and set aside.

2. Combine cornmeal, cumin, $\frac{1}{4}$ teaspoon salt and 1 cup Cheddar cheese in medium bowl. Beat 1 egg, water and oil in small bowl until blended. Stir into cornmeal mixture just until moistened. Pat mixture evenly on bottom and up side of greased 9-inch glass pie plate.

3. Combine remaining 3 eggs, cottage cheese, milk, remaining $\frac{1}{2}$ teaspoon salt and black pepper in blender; cover and blend until smooth.

4. Arrange half of potatoes in crust. Sprinkle with green chiles and $\frac{1}{2}$ cup Cheddar cheese. Top with remaining potatoes and $\frac{1}{2}$ cup Cheddar cheese. Sprinkle with bell pepper strips; pour egg mixture over top.

5. Cover completely with plastic wrap, folding ends under. Place round metal cooling rack inside wok; fill wok with $1\frac{1}{2}$ inches water. (Water should not touch rack.) Place pie plate on rack. Bring water to a boil over high heat; reduce heat to low. Cover wok; steam 35 to 40 minutes or until egg mixture is set. (Replenish water, if necessary.) Cool 10 minutes before serving.

*Makes 6 servings*

# Stuffed Yellow Squash with Artichokes

    4 yellow winter squash (about 8 ounces each) cut in half lengthwise
    1 tablespoons olive oil
 $^3/_4$ cup finely chopped onion
 $^3/_4$ teaspoon dried oregano
 $1^1/_2$ cups cooked brown or white rice
    1 jar (12 ounces) marinated artichoke hearts, drained and coarsely
       chopped
 $^3/_4$ cup canned navy beans, rinsed and drained
 $^1/_3$ cup mayonnaise
 $^1/_4$ cup chopped parsley
 $^1/_4$ cup grated Parmesan cheese seasoned with garlic and herbs*
 $^1/_2$ teaspoon salt
    1 cup shredded mozzarella cheese

*If seasoned cheese is not available, use plain Parmesan cheese and add
$^1/_4$ teaspoon Italian seasoning and $^1/_4$ teaspoon garlic powder.

1. Preheat oven to 350°F. Remove seeds and flesh from each squash half
with tip of teaspoon. Discard seeds; chop flesh coarsely. Set shells aside.

2. Heat oil in large skillet over medium-high heat. Add chopped squash,
onion and oregano; cook and stir 4 minutes or until onion is translucent.
Remove from heat. Stir in remaining ingredients, except mozzarella. Divide
mixture evenly among squash shells. Place on shells baking sheet. Bake
40 minutes or until squash is tender. Sprinkle evenly with mozzarella. Bake
3 minutes or until cheese is melted.                    *Makes 4 servings*

Variation: Substitute 2 large squash, about 1 pound each, for 4 smaller
squash. Cut each squash in half lengthwise, then cut each section in half
crosswise.

# Satisfying Sides

# Oniony Corn Spoonbread

1 can (14³/₄ ounces) cream-style corn
1 can (11 ounces) Mexican-style corn
1 cup sour cream
1 package (6¹/₂ to 8¹/₂ ounces) corn muffin mix
¹/₂ cup diced red and green bell pepper
1 large egg
2 tablespoons butter or margarine, melted
1¹/₃ cups *French's*® French Fried Onions, divided
¹/₂ cup (2 ounces) shredded Cheddar cheese
    Garnish: red bell pepper and chopped parsley (optional)

1. Preheat oven to 350°F. Combine corn, sour cream, corn muffin mix, bell peppers, egg, butter and ²/₃ *cup* French Fried Onions. Pour mixture into greased shallow 2-quart baking dish.

2. Bake 40 minutes or until set. Top with cheese and remaining onions; bake 5 minutes or until onions are golden. Garnish with bell pepper and parsley, if desired.                           *Makes 8 servings*

Variation: For added Cheddar flavor, substitute *French's*® *Cheddar French Fried Onions* for the original flavor.

Prep Time: 5 minutes
Cook Time: 45 minutes

# Wild Mushroom Baked Beans

1 package (3.5 ounces) fresh shiitake mushrooms, sliced

1 package (8 ounces) baby bella mushrooms, sliced

1 cup chopped onion

2 teaspoons minced garlic

2 tablespoons olive oil

2 tablespoons flour

1 can (15 ounces) pinto beans *or* 1$^1$/$_2$ cups cooked, dry-packaged pinto beans, rinsed and drained

1 can (15 ounces) Great Northern beans *or* 1$^1$/$_2$ cups cooked, dry-packaged Great Northern beans, rinsed and drained

1 can (15 ounces) red kidney beans *or* 1$^1$/$_2$ cups cooked, dry-packaged red kidney beans, rinsed and drained

1$^1$/$_2$ cups dry white wine or vegetable broth

$^3$/$_4$ teaspoon dried thyme leaves

Finely chopped parsley

Sauté mushrooms, onion, and garlic in oil in large skillet until tender, about 8 to 10 minutes. Stir in flour; cook 1 to 2 minutes.

Combine mushroom mixture and remaining ingredients except parsley in 2-quart casserole. Bake uncovered, at 350°F 45 minutes. Sprinkle with parsley before serving.

*Makes 6 main-dish (1-cup) servings or 12 side-dish ($^1$/$_2$-cup) servings*

Substitution: **Any wild or domestic mushroom can be used in this recipe.**

Substitution: **Any canned or dry-packaged bean variety can be easily substituted for another.**

Prep Time: **15 to 20 minutes**

Bake Time: **45 minutes**

Favorite recipe from **American Dry Bean Board**

Satisfying Sides

# Carrie's Sweet Potato Casserole

Topping (recipe follows)
3 pounds sweet potatoes, cooked and peeled*
$\frac{1}{2}$ cup (1 stick) butter, softened
$\frac{1}{2}$ cup granulated sugar
$\frac{1}{2}$ cup evaporated milk
2 eggs
1 teaspoon vanilla
1 cup chopped pecans

*For faster preparation, substitute canned sweet potatoes.

**1.** Preheat oven to 350°F. Grease 8 (6-ounce) ovenproof ramekins or 13×9-inch baking dish. Prepare Topping; set aside.

**2.** Mash sweet potatoes and butter in large bowl. Beat with electric mixer at medium speed until light and fluffy.

**3.** Add granulated sugar, evaporated milk, eggs and vanilla, beating after each addition. Spread evenly in prepared ramekins. Spoon Topping over potatoes; sprinkle with pecans.

**4.** Bake 20 to 25 minutes or until set.                    *Makes 8 servings*

Topping: Combine 1 cup packed brown sugar, $\frac{1}{2}$ cup all-purpose flour and $\frac{1}{3}$ cup melted butter in medium bowl; stir until well blended.

# Southwest Spaghetti Squash

1 spaghetti squash (about 3 pounds)
1 can (about 14 ounces) Mexican-style diced tomatoes
1 can (about 14 ounces) black beans, rinsed and drained
$^3/_4$ cup (3 ounces) shredded Monterey Jack cheese, divided
$^1/_4$ cup finely chopped cilantro
1 teaspoon ground cumin
$^1/_4$ teaspoon garlic salt
$^1/_4$ teaspoon black pepper

1. Preheat oven to 350°F. Spray baking pan and 1$^1/_2$-quart baking dish with nonstick cooking spray. Cut squash in half lengthwise. Remove and discard seeds. Place squash, cut side down, in prepared baking pan. Bake 45 minutes to 1 hour or just until tender. Shred hot squash with fork; place in large bowl. (Use oven mitts to protect hands.)

2. Add tomatoes, beans, $^1/_2$ cup cheese, cilantro, cumin, garlic salt and pepper; toss well. Spoon mixture into prepared dish. Sprinkle with remaining $^1/_4$ cup cheese.

3. Bake, uncovered, 30 to 35 minutes or until heated through.

*Makes 4 servings*

Tip: This is a simple, kid-friendly dish you can throw together in a few minutes. It's great for those nights you want to go meatless!

# Scalloped Potatoes with Gorgonzola

1 (14$\frac{1}{2}$-ounce) can chicken broth
1$\frac{1}{2}$ cups whipping cream
4 teaspoons minced garlic
1$\frac{1}{2}$ teaspoons dried sage leaves
1 cup BELGIOIOSO® Gorgonzola Cheese
2$\frac{1}{4}$ pounds russet potatoes, peeled, halved and thinly sliced
Salt and pepper to taste

Preheat oven to 375°F. In medium heavy saucepan, simmer chicken broth, whipping cream, garlic and sage 5 minutes or until slightly thickened. Add BelGioioso® Gorgonzola Cheese and stir until melted. Remove from heat.

Place potatoes in large bowl and season with salt and pepper. Arrange half of potatoes in 13×9×2-inch glass baking dish. Pour half of cream mixture over top of potatoes. Repeat layers with remaining potatoes and cream mixture. Bake until potatoes are tender, about 1$\frac{1}{4}$ hours. Let stand 15 minutes before serving.　　　*Makes 8 servings*

# Sesame-Honey Vegetable Casserole

1 package (16 ounces) frozen mixed vegetable medley, such as baby
    carrots, broccoli, onions and red bell peppers, thawed and drained
3 tablespoons honey
1 tablespoon dark sesame oil
1 tablespoon soy sauce
2 teaspoons sesame seeds

1. Preheat oven to 350°F. Place vegetables in shallow 1½-quart casserole dish.

2. Combine honey, sesame oil, soy sauce and sesame seeds in small bowl; stir until well blended. Drizzle evenly over vegetables.

3. Bake 20 to 25 minutes or until vegetables are tender and heated through, stirring after 15 minutes. *Makes 4 to 6 servings*

This recipe can also be made with fresh vegetables. Make sure to cut vegetables into similar bite-sized pieces. Just add 5 minutes to cooking time and bake until veggies are crisp-tender.

# White Bean and Ripe Olive Gratin

2 tablespoons olive oil
1 cup thinly sliced celery
$\frac{1}{2}$ cup thinly sliced red onion
1 teaspoon minced garlic
2 cups seeded, diced Roma tomatoes
2 cups diced zucchini ($\frac{1}{4}$-inch)
2 cups sliced California Ripe Olives
$\frac{1}{4}$ cup chopped fresh sage
2 (15-ounce) cans white beans, rinsed
1 cup fresh bread crumbs
1 teaspoon minced garlic
$\frac{1}{4}$ cup chopped parsley
1 teaspoon lemon zest
2 tablespoons olive oil

Preheat oven to 350°F. Heat olive oil in heavy pot. Add celery, onion and garlic. Sauté over medium-high heat 3 minutes. Add tomatoes and zucchini and simmer for 5 minutes. Remove from heat. Add olives and sage. Puree about $\frac{1}{4}$ of the beans and add all beans to tomato mixture. Mix well and adjust seasoning with salt and pepper. Transfer to a buttered 2-quart shallow baking dish. Combine the last five ingredients in small bowl. Mix well and sprinkle evenly over casserole. Bake at 350°F until bubbly and golden, about 45 minutes. Let rest 5 to 10 minutes before serving.

*Makes 8 servings*

Favorite recipe from **California Olive Industry**

# Baked Tomato Risotto

1 jar (28 ounces) pasta sauce
2 cups sliced zucchini
1 can (about 14 ounces) chicken broth
1 cup arborio rice
1 can (4 ounces) sliced mushrooms, drained
2 cups (8 ounces) shredded mozzarella cheese

**1.** Preheat oven to 350°F. Spray 3-quart casserole with nonstick cooking spray.

**2.** Combine pasta sauce, zucchini, chicken broth, rice and mushrooms in prepared dish.

**3.** Cover; bake 30 minutes. Remove from oven; stir. Cover; bake 15 to 20 minutes or until rice is tender. Remove from oven; sprinkle evenly with cheese. Bake, uncovered, 5 minutes or until cheese is melted.

*Makes 6 servings*

Although this is not the traditional way to make risotto, it's the perfect side dish for any meal. The rice should be tender and flavorful at the end of cook time.

# Party Potatoes

1 bag (32 ounces) Southern-style hash browns
2 cans (10¾ ounces each) condensed cream of potato soup, undiluted
1 container (16 ounces) sour cream
2 cups (8 ounces) shredded Cheddar cheese
¾ cup finely chopped red onion
¼ cup (½ stick) butter, cut into pieces
   Parmesan cheese (optional)

1. Preheat oven to 350°F. Grease 13×9-inch baking dish.

2. Combine hash browns, soup, sour cream, Cheddar cheese and onion in large bowl. Spoon evenly into baking dish and pat down. Dot with butter; sprinkle with Parmesan cheese, if desired.

3. Cover with foil; bake 50 minutes. Remove foil; bake 20 minutes or until browned.                                    *Makes 10 servings*

# Acorn Squash with Corn Bread Stuffing

1 acorn squash (about 2 pounds)
$^1/_4$ cup ($^1/_2$ stick) butter, divided
2 cups chopped mushrooms
1 medium onion, chopped
1 stalk celery, chopped
$^3/_4$ cup seasoned corn bread stuffing mix
$^1/_4$ teaspoon salt
$^1/_4$ teaspoon black pepper
2 tablespoons packed brown sugar, divided

1. Preheat oven to 375°F. Cut squash into quarters; remove and discard seeds. Place squash, skin side up, in microwavable dish; add $^1/_2$ inch water. Cover loosely with plastic wrap; microwave on HIGH 8 to 10 minutes or until tender.* Drain well.

2. Meanwhile, melt 2 tablespoons butter in large saucepan over medium heat. Add mushrooms, onion and celery; cook and stir 7 to 10 minutes or until tender. Remove from heat. Stir in stuffing mix, salt and pepper.

3. Place squash in baking dish, cut-side up. Top each quarter with $1^1/_2$ teaspoons butter and $1^1/_2$ teaspoons brown sugar. Pack $^1/_2$ cup stuffing onto each quarter. Bake 25 to 30 minutes or until stuffing is golden brown.

*Makes 4 servings*

*To cook on stovetop, place squash quarters in large saucepan with boiling water to cover. Cook 30 minutes or until fork tender. Drain well.

# Scalloped Sweet Potatoes

4 medium to large sweet potatoes (2 pounds)
4 strips bacon
1 small onion, chopped
$2\frac{1}{2}$ tablespoons all-purpose flour
$\frac{1}{2}$ teaspoon salt
$\frac{1}{4}$ teaspoon black pepper
2 cups milk
$1\frac{1}{4}$ cups grated Parmesan cheese

1. Preheat oven to 325°F. Peel potatoes; cut into $\frac{1}{4}$-inch slices. Place sweet potatoes in large saucepan with enough water to cover; bring to a boil. Boil 5 to 10 minutes or until tender; drain and set aside.

2. Meanwhile, fry bacon in large skillet over medium-high heat until crisp. Remove bacon; drain on paper towel. Crumble and set aside. Add onion to same skillet; cook and stir 5 minutes or until tender. Reduce heat; add flour, cooking and stirring until paste forms. Add salt and pepper. Increase heat to medium. Add milk; cook and stir until mixture thickens slightly.

3. Arrange half of sweet potatoes in bottom of 11×7-inch baking dish. Sprinkle with half of bacon. Pour half of milk mixture over bacon. Top with remaining sweet potatoes; sprinkle with remaining bacon. Pour remaining milk mixture over top. Sprinkle with cheese. Bake 20 minutes or until potatoes are tender.                                   *Makes 8 servings*

Tip: If preparing in advance, bake as directed. Cover and refrigerate up to one day. Reheat 15 minutes, covered, at 325°F. Uncover; heat 5 minutes or until heated through.

# Broccoli Casserole with Crumb Topping

2 slices day-old white bread, coarsely crumbled (about 1$\frac{1}{4}$ cups)
$\frac{1}{2}$ cup shredded mozzarella cheese (about 2 ounces)
2 tablespoons chopped fresh parsley (optional)
2 tablespoons BERTOLLI® Olive Oil, divided
1 clove garlic, finely chopped
6 cups broccoli florets and/or cauliflowerets
1 envelope LIPTON® RECIPE SECRETS® Onion Soup Mix
1 cup water
1 large tomato, chopped

**1.** In small bowl, combine bread crumbs, cheese, parsley, 1 tablespoon oil and garlic; set aside.

**2.** In 12-inch skillet, heat remaining 1 tablespoon oil over medium heat and cook broccoli, stirring frequently, 2 minutes.

**3.** Stir in soup mix blended with water. Bring to a boil over high heat. Reduce heat to low and simmer uncovered, stirring occasionally, 8 minutes or until broccoli is almost tender. Add tomato and simmer 2 minutes.

**4.** Spoon vegetable mixture into 1$\frac{1}{2}$-quart casserole; top with bread crumb mixture. Broil 1$\frac{1}{2}$ minutes or until crumbs are golden and cheese is melted.

*Makes 6 servings*

# Spinach and Potatoes Au Gratin

4 medium red potatoes, cut into $1/4$-inch slices
1 bag (8 to 9 ounces) baby spinach*
2 tablespoons melted butter
$1/4$ teaspoon salt, divided
$1/8$ teaspoon black pepper, divided
$1/2$ cup whipping cream
    Pinch ground nutmeg
$1/2$ cup grated Parmesan cheese

*You may substitute regular spinach, but remove tough stems after washing.*

1. Preheat oven to 350°F. Grease medium baking dish; arrange half of potato slices in dish.

2. Place spinach in large saucepan; add water to cover. Bring to a boil. Boil 1 minute; drain. Rinse under cold water; squeeze out excess moisture. Place half of spinach on potato slices. Drizzle with melted butter. Sprinkle with salt and pepper. Repeat layers. Combine cream and nutmeg in small bowl; pour over spinach.

3. Bake 40 to 50 minutes or until potatoes are crisp-tender. Remove from oven; sprinkle with cheese. Bake 15 minutes or until cheese is lightly browned and potatoes are tender. If cheese browns too quickly, cover lightly with foil and finish baking.                    *Makes 6 servings*

# Corn Pudding

1 tablespoon butter
1 small onion, chopped
1 tablespoon all-purpose flour
2 cups half-and-half
1 cup milk
$\frac{1}{4}$ cup quick-cooking grits or polenta
$\frac{3}{4}$ teaspoon salt
$\frac{1}{4}$ teaspoon black pepper
$\frac{1}{4}$ teaspoon hot pepper sauce
2 cups fresh or thawed frozen corn
1 can (4 ounces) diced mild chiles, drained
4 eggs, lightly beaten

1. Preheat oven to 325°F. Grease 11×7-inch baking dish.

2. Melt butter in large saucepan over medium heat. Add onion; cook and stir 5 minutes or until tender and light golden brown. Stir in flour; cook until golden brown. Stir in half-and-half and milk. Bring to a boil. Whisk in grits; reduce heat to medium-low. Cook and stir 10 minutes or until mixture is thickened.

3. Remove from heat. Stir in salt, black pepper and hot pepper sauce. Add corn and chiles. Stir in eggs. Pour into prepared dish. Bake 1 hour or until knife inserted into center comes out clean.          *Makes 8 servings*

Potluck Tip: If preparing in advance, bake pudding as directed. Cover and refrigerate up to one day. To serve, microwave until heated through. Or wrap baked dish in several layers of aluminum foil and overwrap with thick towel or newspapers to keep finished dish warm while transporting.

# Zucchini with Feta Casserole

4 medium zucchini, peeled
2 teaspoons butter or margarine
$1/2$ cup grated Parmesan cheese
2 eggs, beaten
$1/3$ cup crumbled feta cheese
2 tablespoons chopped fresh parsley
1 tablespoon all-purpose flour
2 teaspoons chopped fresh marjoram
Dash hot pepper sauce
Salt and black pepper to taste

1. Preheat oven to 375°F. Grease 2-quart casserole.

2. Grate zucchini; drain in colander. Melt butter in medium skillet over medium heat. Add zucchini; cook and stir until slightly browned. Remove from heat.

3. Add remaining ingredients to skillet; mix well.

4. Pour into prepared casserole. Bake 35 minutes or until bubbly and heated through. *Makes 4 servings*

# Potatoes and Leeks au Gratin

5 tablespoons butter, divided

2 large leeks, sliced

2 tablespoons minced garlic

2 pounds baking potatoes, peeled (about 4 medium), cut into
   thin slices

1 cup whipping cream

1 cup milk

3 eggs

2 teaspoons salt

$1/4$ teaspoon white pepper

2 to 3 slices dense day-old white bread, such as French or Italian

2 ounces grated Parmesan cheese

   Fresh herbs for garnish

1. Preheat oven to 375°F. Generously grease shallow $2\frac{1}{2}$-quart baking dish with 1 tablespoon butter; set aside.

2. Melt 2 tablespoons butter in large skillet over medium heat. Add leeks and garlic; cook and stir 8 to 10 minutes or until leeks are tender. Remove from heat; set aside.

3. Layer half of potato slices in prepared baking dish. Top with half of leek mixture. Repeat layers. Whisk cream, milk, eggs, salt and white pepper in medium bowl until well blended; pour evenly over leeks.

4. Tear bread slices into small pieces and place in food processor; process until fine crumbs form. Measure $3/4$ cup crumbs; place in small bowl. Stir in Parmesan cheese. Melt remaining 2 tablespoons butter. Add to crumb mixture; stir. Sprinkle crumb mixture evenly over vegetables in baking dish.

5. Bake 50 to 60 minutes or until top is golden brown and potatoes are tender. Let stand 5 to 10 minutes before serving.

*Makes 6 to 8 servings*

# Curried Cauliflower & Cashews

1 medium head cauliflower, broken into florets (about 4 cups)
$\frac{1}{2}$ cup water
$\frac{3}{4}$ cup toasted unsalted cashews
3 tablespoons butter, divided
2 tablespoons all-purpose flour
1 tablespoon curry powder
$1\frac{1}{4}$ cups milk
Salt and black pepper
1 cup dry bread crumbs
Additional toasted unsalted cashews, for garnish

1. Preheat oven to 350°F. Grease 2-quart casserole.

2. Place cauliflower in large microwavable dish. Add water; microwave on HIGH about 4 minutes or until crisp-tender. Drain; transfer to prepared casserole. Stir $\frac{3}{4}$ cup cashews.

3. Melt 2 tablespoons butter in medium saucepan. Add flour and curry powder; cook and stir 2 minutes over medium heat. Whisk in milk; cook and stir until mixture thickens slightly. Season with salt and pepper.

4. Pour milk mixture over cauliflower mixture; stir to coat. Sprinkle with bread crumbs. Dot with remaining 1 tablespoon butter.

5. Bake 45 minutes or until lightly browned. Garnish as desired.

*Makes 8 servings*

# Potatoes au Gratin

4 to 6 medium unpeeled baking potatoes (about 2 pounds), cut into thin slices
2 cups (8 ounces) shredded Cheddar cheese
1 cup (4 ounces) shredded Swiss cheese
2 tablespoons butter
3 tablespoons all-purpose flour
2½ cups milk
2 tablespoons Dijon mustard
¼ teaspoon salt
¼ teaspoon black pepper

1. Preheat oven to 400°F. Grease 13×9-inch baking dish.

2. Layer potatoes in prepared dish. Top with cheeses.

3. Melt butter in medium saucepan over medium heat. Stir in flour; cook 1 minute. Stir in milk, mustard, salt and pepper; bring to a boil. Reduce heat; cook, stirring constantly, until mixture thickens. Pour milk mixture over cheese.

4. Cover with foil; bake 30 minutes. Remove foil; bake 15 to 20 minutes or until potatoes are tender and top is browned. Let stand 10 minutes before serving. *Makes 6 to 8 servings*

# Summer Squash Casserole

2 cups sliced yellow squash

1 medium carrot, thinly sliced

½ cup chopped onion

½ cup diced red or green bell pepper

½ teaspoon salt

⅛ teaspoon black pepper

1 can (10¾ ounces) condensed cream of chicken or mushroom soup, undiluted

1 container (8 ounces) sour cream

1 cup (4 ounces) shredded Italian cheese blend

1 cup (4 ounces) shredded Cheddar cheese

1 package (6 ounces) stuffing mix

**1.** Preheat oven to 350°F. Combine squash, carrot, onion, bell pepper, salt and black pepper in medium saucepan; cover with water. Bring to a boil. Cook 5 minutes or until tender; drain.

**2.** Combine soup and sour cream in 13×9-inch baking dish; mix well. Spread vegetable mixture evenly over soup mixture. Sprinkle evenly with cheeses.

**3.** Top with stuffing mix. Cover; bake 30 minutes or until heated through.

*Makes 6 servings*

# Creamy Spinach Italiano

1 cup ricotta cheese

$^3/_4$ cup half-and-half or milk

2 packages (10 ounces each) frozen chopped spinach, thawed and squeezed dry

1$^1/_3$ cups *French's*® French Fried Onions, divided

$^1/_2$ cup chopped roasted red pepper

$^1/_4$ cup chopped fresh basil

$^1/_4$ cup grated Parmesan cheese

1 teaspoon garlic powder

$^1/_4$ teaspoon salt

1. Preheat oven to 350°F. Whisk together ricotta cheese and half-and-half in large bowl until well combined. Stir in spinach, $^2/_3$ *cup* French Fried Onions, red pepper, basil, Parmesan, garlic powder and salt. Pour mixture into greased deep-dish casserole.

2. Bake for 25 minutes or until heated through; stir. Sprinkle with remaining $^2/_3$ *cup* onions. Bake for 5 minutes or until onions are golden.

*Makes 4 servings*

Prep Time: **10 minutes**
Cook Time: **35 minutes**

# Vegetable Gratin

2 tablespoons olive oil
3 small *or* 1 large zucchini, cut into $1/4$-inch slices
$1/8$ teaspoon salt, divided
$1/8$ teaspoon thyme, divided
$1/8$ teaspoon rosemary, divided
$1/8$ teaspoon freshly ground black pepper, divided
1 (6.5-ounce) package ALOUETTE® Savory Vegetable Spreadable Cheese
2 cups fresh broccoli florets
2 small yellow squash, sliced
1 small onion, sliced
1 cup crushed BRETON® Wheat Crackers

• Preheat oven to 350°F. Place oil in medium-sized gratin or shallow baking dish.

• Layer zucchini in prepared dish.

• Sprinkle zucchini lightly with half each of salt, thyme, rosemary and pepper.

• Place 3 tablespoons Alouette® on top of zucchini.

• Layer with broccoli, yellow squash, onion, remaining seasonings and Alouette® until dish is filled.

• Sprinkle with cracker crumbs; cover with foil. Bake 20 minutes.

• Remove foil; bake another 20 minutes. Brown lightly under broiler 1 to 2 minutes. Serve hot or at room temperature.        *Makes 6 to 8 servings*

Note: This gratin is a delicious way to liven up vegetables! It's great with grilled chicken or steak.

# Crunchy Top & Flaky Bottom Broccoli Casserole

2 cans (8 ounces each) refrigerated crescent roll dough

1 package (16 ounces) frozen chopped broccoli

2 cups (8 ounces) shredded mozzarella cheese, divided

1½ cups French fried onions, coarsely crushed and divided

1 can (10¾ ounces) condensed cream of mushroom soup, undiluted

2 cans (5 ounces each) lean ham, drained and flaked

½ cup mayonnaise

2 eggs, beaten

2 tablespoons Dijon mustard

1 tablespoon prepared horseradish

1 jar (2 ounces) chopped pimientos, drained

1 teaspoon finely chopped fresh parsley

1. Preheat oven to 375°F. Grease bottom of 13×9-inch baking dish. Unroll dough; do not separate. Press dough onto bottom of prepared baking dish, sealing all seams. Bake 7 minutes; remove from oven and set aside.

2. Combine broccoli, 1 cup cheese, ½ cup onions, soup, ham, mayonnaise, eggs, mustard and horseradish. Spread evenly over crust. Top with remaining 1 cup onions, 1 cup cheese, pimientos and parsley.

3. Bake 20 to 25 minutes or until set. Cool 10 minutes before serving.

*Makes 8 servings*

# Polynesian Baked Beans

2 tablespoons olive oil
3 tablespoons chopped onion
2 cans (16 ounces each) baked beans
1 can (about 11 ounces) mandarin oranges, drained
1 can (about 8 ounces) pineapple chunks in juice, drained
$\frac{1}{2}$ cup chopped green bell pepper
1 can (about 4 ounces) deviled ham
$\frac{1}{4}$ cup ketchup
2 tablespoons packed brown sugar
$\frac{1}{2}$ teaspoon salt (optional)
  Dash hot pepper sauce

**1.** Preheat oven to 375°F. Heat oil in small skillet over medium heat. Add onion; cook and stir until translucent.

**2.** Combine onion and remaining ingredients in 2-quart casserole. Bake, uncovered, 30 to 35 minutes or until bubbly and heated through.

*Makes 6 to 8 servings*

Note: This is a great recipe to double; it can also be made in a slow cooker.

# Macaroni & Cheese with Bacon

3 cups (8 ounces) uncooked rotini pasta
2 tablespoons butter or margarine
2 tablespoons all-purpose flour
$\frac{1}{4}$ teaspoon salt
$\frac{1}{4}$ teaspoon dry mustard
$\frac{1}{8}$ teaspoon black pepper
$1\frac{1}{2}$ cups milk
2 cups (8 ounces) shredded sharp Cheddar cheese
8 ounces bacon, crisp-cooked and crumbled*
2 medium tomatoes, sliced

*1 cup cubed cooked ham can be substituted for bacon.

1. Preheat oven to 350°F. Lightly grease $1\frac{1}{2}$-quart shallow casserole.

2. Cook pasta according to package directions; drain and return to saucepan.

3. Melt butter in 2-quart saucepan over medium-low heat. Whisk in flour, salt, mustard and pepper; cook and stir 1 minute. Whisk in milk. Bring to a boil over medium heat, stirring frequently. Reduce heat and simmer 2 minutes. Remove from heat. Add cheese; stir until melted.

4. Add cheese mixture and bacon to pasta; stir until well blended. Transfer to prepared casserole. Bake uncovered 20 minutes. Arrange tomato slices on casserole. Bake additional 5 to 8 minutes or until casserole is bubbly and tomatoes are hot. *Makes 4 servings*

# Acknowledgments

The publisher would like to thank the companies listed below
for the use of their recipes in this publication.

Allen Canning Company

Alouette® Cheese, Chavrie® Cheese, Saladena®, Montrachet®

BelGioioso® Cheese Inc.

California Olive Industry

Del Monte Corporation

Florida Department of Agriculture and Consumer Services, Bureau of
Seafood and Aquaculture

Hillshire Farm®

Hormel Foods, LLC

MASTERFOODS USA

National Cattlemen's Beef Association on Behalf of The Beef Checkoff

National Chicken Council / US Poultry & Egg Association

Norseland, Inc.

North Dakota Wheat Commission

Ortega®, A Division of B&G Foods, Inc.

Reckitt Benckiser Inc.

Unilever

US Dry Bean Council

Veg•All®

Index

249

# METRIC CONVERSION CHART

## VOLUME MEASUREMENTS (dry)

1/8 teaspoon = 0.5 mL
1/4 teaspoon = 1 mL
1/2 teaspoon = 2 mL
3/4 teaspoon = 4 mL
1 teaspoon = 5 mL
1 tablespoon = 15 mL
2 tablespoons = 30 mL
1/4 cup = 60 mL
1/3 cup = 75 mL
1/2 cup = 125 mL
2/3 cup = 150 mL
3/4 cup = 175 mL
1 cup = 250 mL
2 cups = 1 pint = 500 mL
3 cups = 750 mL
4 cups = 1 quart = 1 L

## VOLUME MEASUREMENTS (fluid)

1 fluid ounce (2 tablespoons) = 30 mL
4 fluid ounces (1/2 cup) = 125 mL
8 fluid ounces (1 cup) = 250 mL
12 fluid ounces (1 1/2 cups) = 375 mL
16 fluid ounces (2 cups) = 500 mL

## WEIGHTS (mass)

1/2 ounce = 15 g
1 ounce = 30 g
3 ounces = 90 g
4 ounces = 120 g
8 ounces = 225 g
10 ounces = 285 g
12 ounces = 360 g
16 ounces = 1 pound = 450 g

## DIMENSIONS

1/16 inch = 2 mm
1/8 inch = 3 mm
1/4 inch = 6 mm
1/2 inch = 1.5 cm
3/4 inch = 2 cm
1 inch = 2.5 cm

## OVEN TEMPERATURES

250°F = 120°C
275°F = 140°C
300°F = 150°C
325°F = 160°C
350°F = 180°C
375°F = 190°C
400°F = 200°C
425°F = 220°C
450°F = 230°C

## BAKING PAN SIZES

| Utensil | Size in Inches/Quarts | Metric Volume | Size in Centimeters |
|---|---|---|---|
| Baking or Cake Pan (square or rectangular) | 8×8×2 | 2 L | 20×20×5 |
| | 9×9×2 | 2.5 L | 23×23×5 |
| | 12×8×2 | 3 L | 30×20×5 |
| | 13×9×2 | 3.5 L | 33×23×5 |
| Loaf Pan | 8×4×3 | 1.5 L | 20×10×7 |
| | 9×5×3 | 2 L | 23×13×7 |
| Round Layer Cake Pan | 8×1½ | 1.2 L | 20×4 |
| | 9×1½ | 1.5 L | 23×4 |
| Pie Plate | 8×1¼ | 750 mL | 20×3 |
| | 9×1¼ | 1 L | 23×3 |
| Baking Dish or Casserole | 1 quart | 1 L | — |
| | 1½ quart | 1.5 L | — |
| | 2 quart | 2 L | |